796.3331   SbN
9.11.70

D E
/eJR   35/=

X

2.2.

RUGBY: MEN, MATCHES
AND MOMENTS

RUGBY: MEN, MATCHES
AND MOMENTS

Impressions of the Game in the
Post-War Years
by
J. B. G. Thomas

PELHAM BOOKS

First published in Great Britain by
PELHAM BOOKS LTD
*52 Bedford Square
London, W.C.*1
1970

7207 0051 5

*Printed in Great Britain by Northumberland
Press Limited, Gateshead in eleven on
thirteen point Baskerville, and bound by The
Dorstel Press, Harlow, Essex*

To Craig—Wayne—Gareth

CONTENTS

ILLUSTRATIONS

ACKNOWLEDGEMENTS

The author's thanks are due to the following whose photographs are reproduced in this book as indicated: *Western Mail*: 1, 2, 10, 17, 22, 23, 24, 26, 27, 29, 31. *Evening Post, Wellington*: 3. *Crown Studios, Wellington*: 4. *Gwyn Martin*: 6, 15, *Sport & General*: 5, 8, 21, 28. *Belfast Telegraph*: 9. *Evening News, Dunedin*: 12. *Mirroir du Rugby*: 13. *Pretoria News*: 14. *Fox Photos*: 18. *Camera Press*: 19. *Cape Argus*: 20. *Keystone Press*: 25. *Sydney Sun*: 30. *Thomson Press*: 33.

PREFACE

Sports writers are often accused of becoming pontifical as they grow older revealing a tendency to talk of the past in preference to the present. At the risk of being thus accused I have recalled in this book memories and impressions gained as a rugby critic since the end of World War II.

Rugby players, administrators and followers are people; to me likeable people; and it is people who matter. Meeting them, watching them and talking to them, and even writing about them with words of praise and criticism has given me much pleasure.

Through the encouragement of the *Western Mail*, the Thomson Organisation, my publishers, magazine and overseas editors, I have been able to study the game at close quarters in many countries. Being an incurable optimist, I have great hopes for the future of the game throughout the world. It has faults but these are outnumbered by the good points and the genuine enthusiasm for it.

This book is intended as a mirror; reflecting a cross-section of the matches, players, administrators and occasions of the post-War years in the game. It is not intended as a complete record or history of the game during this period but about personalities in the game with whom I have shared many happy moments before, during and after 'the match'. They are important, and have played an important part in the development of the game.

However, they are only a few, but representative of the whole. The book is intended as a tribute to all who have done something for the game in the post-War years.

My thanks are due to those who helped so readily when I interviewed them. They were all extremely modest, but it has given me pleasure to sing their praises.

JBGT

PROLOGUE

A Century of Organised Rugby

This book, which has given me so much pleasure to write, has been completed before the start of one of the most important seasons in the game, for England is about to celebrate the Centenary of its Rugby Football Union. Thus one hundred years of organised administration in rugby football will be recalled and honoured as well as one hundred years of international matches. How pleasant it would be to have seen them all and yet remain capable of writing about this new season's many special matches!

So much has happened since the 1870-71 season, that those worthy pioneers of control and organisation would experience something of a shock today were they able to see how the Game has grown, not only in England where it was born and nurtured, but throughout the world. The historic meeting at the Pall Mall Restaurant on January 26, 1871 found 32 people representing 21 Clubs, with E. C. Holmes in the chair, although unfortunately the representatives of the Wasps, a healthy member of the present Rugby Football Union, did not attend the meeting owing to a misunderstanding over the time and place.

Eight of the 21 clubs are still in existence and these will play an important part in the celebrations; the other 12 are now defunct although some of their names sound most romantic. There were the Marlborough Nomads, the Wimbledon Hornets, the Flamingoes, the Mohicans and Belsize Park. At the meeting an annual subscription of 5s. was agreed upon and a committee formed of 13 representatives whose first task was to draw up a set of 'Laws of the Game'.

13

The code of laws was approved on June 22, 1871, and it included 59 items with the last reading, 'The captains of the respective sides shall be the sole arbiters of all disputes.' Let it be known that the rugby 'hardies' of those far off days were truly sporting gentlemen and it was only as the years developed that players even attempted to opt out of the laws when their captains were not watching.

By October 1871, Edinburgh University, Glasgow Academicals and the West of Scotland had joined the Union, and the cash in hand at the first A.G.M. was revealed as eleven shillings. Twenty clubs contributed an income of £10 in subscriptions and the £4. 4s. od. charged for stationery included 20 copies of the first laws of the Game.

The balance sheet of the Rugby Football Union's A.G.M. for 1969-70 revealed an income of £131,015 and a profit on the season's working of £12,278 while it has 1,625 clubs as members and an efficient administrative organisation at Twickenham under a full time secretary qualified in law.

The first international was played between Scotland and England on Monday, March 27, 1871 at the Edinburgh Academy ground at Raeburn Place, and was won by Scotland by a goal and a try to a try. This season Scotland and England will play each other twice, at Murrayfield and at Twickenham, with one match being the normal International Championship fixture and the other to celebrate the centenary of representative football.

Since 1871 many international or test matches have been played in the eight senior countries in the game, England, Scotland, Ireland, Wales, South Africa, New Zealand, Australia and France, and each country has enjoyed its moments of triumph. Strange as it may appear, Wales have never beaten South Africa and Ireland have never defeated New Zealand, but each other country has enjoyed success at the expense of the others.

Since 1871 England have played 85 matches against Scotland with 41 wins against 30; 82 matches against Ireland with 48 victories against 26; 74 against Wales with 32 victories against 32, and 45 against France with 28 victories against 13. Since all four countries first played each other in a season England has beaten all four to achieve the Grand Slam on seven occasions, while the Triple Crown has been won 13 times and the Championship of the Five Nations outright on 16 occasions.

Touring teams from overseas have been beaten at Twickenham and this Centenary season will see a visit from the attractive Fijians playing a series of matches in England and there will be special matches played by a President's XV composed of players from Australia, France, New Zealand, South Africa and perhaps other countries. Such a galaxy of talent playing together at one time will not have been seen in the British Isles before and one imagines that after the Fijians have played their 13 matches, at all the main centres including one against the Barbarians at Gosforth, the whole of England will be alight with the fervour of rugby celebration.

The President elect of the RFU, its honorary treasurer W. C. 'Bill' Ramsay, whose career in the game is referred to, in detail, later in this book, will have an extremely busy year and the Union has prepared a detailed programme of events, dinners and special publications to commemorate the occasion. More important still, they have arranged for a World Rugby Union Congress to be staged at Corpus Christi College, Cambridge and 70 delegates of 'differing colours, creeds and political persuasions' will attend to pursue the 'Development and Enjoyment of the Game'.

Rugby Union football is a special game; born in 1823 at Rugby School, and there have been many celebrations in the past associated with its development, but this season is a most important one. The Centenary Match of 1923 at Rugby School and the 50 years at Twickenham match in 1959 were notable affairs but the big matches this winter are really special.

The President's XV will play matches at Leicester, Birkenhead Park, and Bristol before meeting England at Twickenham on April 17, 1971; after this match there will be a celebration dinner to which approximately 1,000 male guests will be invited. Her Majesty the Queen is expected to attend this match and unveil a commemorative plaque as Patron of the Rugby Football Union. It will be one of the great days in the history of the Game.

Since 1871 many outstanding players have appeared in the ranks of the England side and several are mentioned in this book of memories dealing with the post-War years, but one thinks, too, of Stokes, Guillemard, MacLaren, Green, Birkett, Sherrard and others in that first England side of twenty members. They have been followed by so many more and Rogers, Wakefield, Evans, Cove-Smith, Jacobs, Weston, Butterfield, Voyce, Tucker and Lowe are at the head of the honours list, but one must not forget Rotherham and Bromet, and Woods, Byrne and Jackett; and Stoop and Palmer, and the legendary Temple Gurdon, while Davies and Kershaw, Pillman, Corbett and Young; the second row pair of Marques and Currie, and Jeeps and Jackson. So many fine names; so many rugby heroes, and so difficult to name the greatest of them.

All played the game in the right spirit and helped it, not to survive a hundred years, but to develop and grow; to become more popular than ever as an amateur team game. Administratively, it has had notable officials to guide its fortunes and one thinks of Rowland-Hill, Marriott, Coopper and Prentice, before Robin Prescott, as secretaries of the RFU and honorary treasurers like Wallace, Cail, Prescott (father of Robin) and Ramsay (president for a second time), who have ensured a happy bank balance and the use of profits for the development of clubs playing the game for the love of it. The many presidents down through the years; the official union staff; club secretaries; referees and groundsmen, and all the voluntary workers together with those players whose names never have and never will reach the columns of the national press. Everyone living can enjoy the Centenary and set the game on its true course for the next 100 years. The Games goes on!

PART ONE

The Administrators

Twelve 'Alickadoos'

Tommy Vile

There have been few administrators to achieve almost everything in the game, both on and off the field, and few former internationals who have become outstanding referees and administrators. Most internationals, after retiring from the field of play with honour, have admitted that refereeing is harder than playing! Many former internationals have argued that it is difficult enough to get a cap but more difficult to win a seat on one's rugby union, especially in Wales. Yet there was one remarkable exception, Major Thomas Henry Vile of Newport who died in 1958, after a lifetime of service to rugby union football, at the age of 75.

Affectionately known as 'Tommy', he was quite a character in every way. Short, dapper, with a puckish twinkle in his eye, he really knew his rugby and it was fascinating to chat with him about the game he loved. Many a time I visited his home to hear him pay tribute to the great players he played with and against; his memories as an international referee; his experiences as a coach; and his theories and beliefs on the game.

He was never 'old fashioned' and disliked those who lived in the past, yet he fought hard at all times to preserve the traditions of the game, its amateur status and its spirit; and he was big enough to acknowledge the good in other countries although immensely proud that he played for Wales and became President of the Welsh Rugby Union.

Tommy was a Newport man, first and last, joining that club at the zenith of its greatness, when he was 17 in 1900—as a forward because he could not get in anywhere else! His first game was for Newport Thirds, and during the match

19

the scrum-half and captain was injured and Tommy took his place.

As he told me, 'I was the smallest forward and was drafted to scrum-half. It was my great chance and from that moment I played in the position for the Second XV and Pill Harriers before graduating to the Newport 1st XV. Soon I was playing with that immaculate outside half, Llewellyn Lloyd.'

The rest with Newport is history, for Tommy played for the club until 1921, a career spanning 21 years, and was in his 38th year when playing his last club match. All the honours came to him during his playing career, for he was captain of Newport in three successive seasons (1909-1912), captain of Wales with eight caps between 1908 and 1921, a member of the 1904 British Lions team and a Barbarian. He would surely have earned many more caps but for the presence of the other genius of the time in the position—R. M. 'Dickie' Owen of Swansea who won 35 caps.

Tommy was a quick, accurate and inventive scrum-half; a thinker and an ideal captain. Naturally, I never saw him play, but two of those critics who did, W. J. Townsend Collins and Goff Morgan, have paid outstanding tributes to his skill. When he retired from the game he became a committee man and a referee, and so expert was he in both fields that he achieved international success. As a referee Tommy was the unobtrusive guide and arbiter, and in popular demand in many countries. There was a knowledge-able air of calm about his approach to the game and always he appeared to help the players in their efforts.

Tommy was not an extrovert with a whistle, for he sought to share the pleasure of flowing rugby, and his deep under-standing of the tactics and laws of the game won him many friends. Especially in England was he popular as a referee and had charge of international and inter-varsity matches and many important club and county matches. One of his most treasured possessions was a photograph of H. M. King George V shaking hands with him before the start of the 1924 England v Scotland match at Twickenham.

Lord Wakefield played many times 'under the whistle' of Tommy Vile and has said much in praise of his friend of former years. Others, too, recall his outstanding ability. Tommy was one of the first referees to doubt the legality of the 'rover' forward in the New Zealand 2-3-2 formation, when he penalised him in 1924-25 for not retiring after putting the ball into the scrummage against Cambridge University. This was to set off a chain reaction that eventually brought about the end of the 2-3-2 formation in the early 1930's.

He went out to the Argentine with the British Touring team in 1927 and when he retired, finally, from the field, he devoted even more energy to the game as an administrator. Elected a Vice-President of the Welsh Rugby Union, he became a representative on the International Board, serving from 1946 to 1953, and once told me: 'The Board will only move slowly, for it is there to protect the game. It will not rush headlong into making changes it may regret.' Yet he was a student of the laws and believed that they should be easy to understand, interpret and, above all, easy to play under. 'The game should never be made too difficult to play!', he argued and, perhaps, would be disappointed at the complexity of the modern game.

In the 1955-56 season he was honoured as President of the Welsh Rugby Union, and during his term of office former secretary Eric Evans died and Bill Clement was appointed. Tommy did much to guide the Union along through the transitional period. Outside of rugby he served public life in many ways and was a successful businessman. He was a justice of the peace, a high sheriff of Monmouthshire, and served on many committees for it was always his desire to 'serve' on and off the field.

As a tactician, Tommy was a great believer in the switching of the point of attack, and was sought after by both senior universities as a coach. 'Move the ball quickly to the wings and get him to work the ball back to mid-field. Stretch the defence. Let the wing kick to the centre and make the forwards run up field to collect and score!'

He impressed upon players the need to master the basic skills and think about the game. As a coach he was ahead of his time, perhaps, but then he was a thinker, a student, and someone who loved perfection in the game. Perfection is hard to achieve, but it should be the target for all. Vile possessed many natural gifts, but he developed them by application and dedication. His name is revered in the game.

John Daniell

The men included in this section were or are remarkable characters in the game. Some of them were remarkable in more than one sport, and John Daniell was one of the most remarkable of this remarkable group! I first saw him in action as the captain of Somerset County Cricket team in the mid-1920's, and then sat beside him to meet him for the first time when Wales played England in a Victory International at Cardiff during the 1945-46 season. In pre-War days I had seen him parading along the touch-line at various grounds with his pipe in the corner of his mouth and his hands clasped behind his back. I had learned much about him from others and wondered at the stories related about him. He was indeed a remarkable man.

At Cardiff in January 1946, I was on demobilisation leave and watching my first international as a civilian since 1939. It was an excellent match, full of running rugby, but more fascinating for me were the comments of this most experienced player and administrator, who was then the President of the Rugby Football Union. They varied from the vitriolic to the magnificent, but they were words of wisdom, astute in their depth of penetration about the finer points of the game. His language was occasionally 'flowery' in the sporting sense, but his wisdom and understanding of what was happening impressed me as few senior observers had done previously. Perhaps it was the realisation of a boyhood ambition to meet this man, John Daniell, known universally as 'The Prophet', that caused me to be so impressed. I had read, while at school, that 'Wakers' regarded him as one of the finest judges of a player he had ever known and, invariably, any choice made by Daniell in selection was always the wisest one.

Born in December, 1878, he was educated at Clifton College and played for the School sides in cricket and rugby during 1895-96-97. He then went on to Cambridge, and at the age of 20 scored 107 against a formidable Lancashire team in 1899, to be awarded his Blue by the illustrious G. L. Jessop. His career at Cambridge was most successful; he played three times against Oxford at rugby and cricket and during his undergraduate days was christened 'The Prophet' and the 'Cheerful Pessimist'.

He first appeared in the County Championship for Somerset in 1898 and on coming down from University, had a spell at schoolmastering before departing to India to take up tea-planting. Daniell returned in 1908 to captain Somerset at cricket and remained their leader until the end of the 1912 season. Before leaving for India he played seven times at forward for England and captained the country on two occasions. On relinquishing the captaincy of the Somerset cricket team in 1913, he became a member of the Rugby Union committee and remained one until 1947. He was Chairman of selectors from 1931 to 1939 and followed this as acting-President of the Union during World War II before being the official President for the first two seasons after the War.

In 1919, after serving in the Army in World War I, he resumed as captain of Somerset C.C. for a further seven years and in 1925, at the age of 46, scored two centuries in a match, against Essex at his beloved Taunton. On retiring from first-class cricket in 1927, he served as an England selector and must be one of the few, if not the only person, to serve his country as an international selector in cricket and rugby at the same time. He did a notable job in helping

Somerset cricket and was their President from 1947 to 1949 and a much beloved man in the County.

Throughout his career in sport he was a genuine competitor and his wisdom in the committee and selection rooms placed him high in the list of officials and administrators who have helped the game's progress. In the 1920's, John Daniell, together with Bim Baxter, Bob Oakes, Jock Hartley and E. W. Roberts, did a magnificent job in ensuring that England were the foremost country of the four home unions. The stories about him are legendary; in addition to his picturesque vocabulary, which immediately cut down people to their bootlaces, he was intolerant of slackers. Yet he possessed an enjoyable sense of humour. On one occasion he was tackled by a fellow international, without the ball. The player said, 'Awfully sorry, John', to which Daniell growled in reply, 'And you will be!' Again, when trying to sign the New Zealander Tom Lowry for Somerset, he realised that Wellington, New Zealand, as a birthplace would not do, and so in the application to the MCC, he wrote for Lowry's birthplace, 'Wellington, Somerset!'

The late Dai Gent, one of the kindest of rugby writers, once described Daniell as being 'blunt, outspoken, uncompromising and delightfully pessimistic'. This may be true, but the tough exterior hid, in the words of his son, 'a very soft heart'. This is proved by an incident in World War I, when a trembling corporal appeared before Captain Daniell requesting urgent compassionate leave. 'He cussed me up hill and down dale,' recalls the corporal, 'sent me on seven days leave, gave me a fiver, and said he would slaughter me if I arrived back late at my unit!' This was the action of a kind man, for Daniell was generous, especially to those who were loyal to his leadership. He was much-travelled, much-admired, often contradictory but always modest; rough of tongue, courageous, intelligent, and born to lead from the front.

No one wrote with a better understanding of John Daniell than the late Robertson-Glasgow, who died just two years after 'The Prophet'. It was Daniell who introduced 'Crusoe' to Somerset cricket while the young man was an undergraduate at Oxford. Whenever the two played together, one as captain and the other as an occasionally wayward yet often brilliant bowler, the conversation between them was generally magnificent! 'Crusoe' recalled these conversations in some of his outstanding essays and he did more than anyone to ensure that sport would never forget the remarkable character, John Daniell, who did so much for his County and Country in rugby football and cricket. He came from Cambridge and I can only recall one man from that University, since the time of Daniell, who has done as much for both codes in the Daniell manner, and he is Wilfred Wooller, of Glamorgan. They have much in common in make-up, for their inspiration, devotion and loyalty have earned for them the admiration of colleagues and opponents alike. All team games are better for outstanding, disciplined and inspired leadership, and the changing face of sport will not alter these necessities!

Walter E. Rees

The late Walter Enoch Rees—the most illustrious of Welsh administrators—became a legend in his own lifetime. He was known to his intimate friends as Walter, and to the populace as Captain Rees. About him a thousand tales can be told and he is remembered in Wales as are players like Owen, Trew, Bancroft, Gabe and Nicholls, for Walter was truly a character; more than that even, an institution in the game. Indeed, until his death in 1949, at the age of 87, he seemed as old as Welsh rugby itself, an ever-present member of the administration. One might even say that he was THE administration for his powerful 52 years as secretary!

Never in the history of rugby football has one man wielded as much power as this benevolent 'dictator', who served rugby faithfully in his native land and maintained a dignity and a control that was the envy of many. He *was* Welsh rugby and not even Danie Craven, the most powerful of modern administrators, can match the influence possessed by Walter at the height of his power, in the days between the Wars.

Many have tried to denigrate this amazing personality; some because they were envious of his power, others because they never understood him, while some felt him pompous because he did not suffer fools gladly. It is true that he had certain weaknesses, as have most benevolent dictators but his fantastic aplomb and capacity to survive in the corridors of rugby power give cause for him to be remembered as one of the most amazing personalities the game has ever known.

He fascinated me always, even before the War when, as a 'beginner in the trade', I approached him rather nervously for a Press pass, and then later when I knew him more intimately, and sat with him in his dining-room at 'Norwood', Neath (which was the WRU office for 52 years) sorting out the Press passes for international matches.

Yes, Walter was an autocrat and ran the Union as he thought fit, but always doing what he thought was in the best interests of Welsh rugby. Whenever I asked awkward questions about the agenda of a monthly meeting of the WRU executive, he used to reply, as we supped a cup of coffee, 'I wouldn't say anything about that!'

Perhaps, in his later years, he took too much upon himself, for immediately before and after World War II he was all-powerful, and it was he who directed affairs under the equally long-serving President, Horace Lyne. When the great administrator from Newport passed away, Sir David Rocyn Jones became President and this dapper, dynamic figure set the Union along a more democratic road. Walter resigned from his post at the great age of 86, the oldest rugby secretary of all time, and no representative official is ever likely to break his record of 52 years unbroken service.

Some of the legendary stories about this remarkable personality make interesting reading. Few rugby officials have been able to commandeer a whole train and, even fewer, able to drive into Twickenham in a magnificent saloon with a police escort of outriders while his committee travelled by coach! No secretary in my lifetime has ever engaged in a 'grand parade' round the touchlines of his home ground, raising his hat to the salute of the crowd. This was Walter, the supremo of Welsh rugby.

He was born at Neath on April 13, 1862, and was first employed as a secretary by the Ministry of Labour before becoming the secretary of the Welsh Rugby Union in 1896 in succession to W. H. Gwynne. At the time he was 34 years of age and did not marry until he was 46, and then to a Scottish lady, Miss Elizabeth Peters, of Aberdeen. Becoming the Union secretary, as he did, a few years after their first Triple Crown triumph, he enjoyed taking an important part in the most colourful period of Welsh rugby, through the 'Golden Era' from 1900 to 1911. When World War I arrived he was too old for active service, and became the recruiting officer for the Neath, Port Talbot and Bridgend areas.

Walter was particularly interested in public life, being elected to the Neath Town Council in 1900 and becoming the town's mayor in the memorable year of 1905. Prior to his becoming the WRU secretary, he had been secretary of the Neath club and a district member of the WRU, as well as a representative on the International Board. Thus he was extremely knowledgeable in the ways of public life and in the administration of the game. When he took office in 1896 there were 50 clubs in the Union, but when he retired in 1948 there were 104. Again, in 1896, the receipts for the Wales v England match at Newport were £1,100, while in 1948 the Scottish game at Cardiff produced nearly £10,000.

Walter was known throughout the rugby world, and in 1910 was one of two managers of the British Lions' team in South Africa. Again, he was Neath's senior magistrate for many years and towards the end of his life carried out his duties bravely while suffering ill-health. Public life to him was the very essence of living and, although he enjoyed the plaudits of the crowd, he was a remarkable administrator. Those who worked with him appreciated this, for he possessed unconquerable energy and enthusiasm.

To the people outside the inner circles of Welsh rugby he will be remembered best as Captain Rees, a short, dapper figure, immaculately dressed, who stood in the foyer of the Queen's Hotel at Cardiff, or the Metropole Hotel at Swansea, on the morning of an international match, producing tickets of admission for late-comers, and particularly those exiled Welshmen who had travelled many miles to see the old country in action.

When he retired, and I was the only other person present when he handed his resignation to Sir David Rocyn Jones over lunch at the Queen's Hotel in Cardiff, he told me with tears in his eyes, 'I have been very happy in the job, which has been full of pleasant memories.'

With the retirement of Walter, and his death a year later, Welsh rugby lost one of its most important figureheads. After his passing there followed an era of change and the establishment of proper Union headquarters in Cardiff. The era of 'benevolent dictatorship' had passed, as have so many other traditions in the game in recent years. Critics of Captain Walter Rees there may have been, but there can be no denying his ability, his power and tremendous influence as a top rugby official. I will remember always his saying to me in Paris in 1947, as we marched through an avenue of gendarmes from Stade Colombes to the official coach in case of crowd troubles, 'Is this a guard of honour for me, Thomas?'

Herbert Waddell

Herbert Waddell has also become a legend in the game in his own lifetime. A remarkable personality, a man of many words, who does not suffer fools gladly. His son, Gordon, who followed him at outside-half for Scotland and into the Lions' team, calls his father 'Napoleon', and in many ways he resembles the famous French commander in his approach to the game.

It is not everyone outside Scotland who enjoys chatting with Waddell Senior, but I do at all times, and it is a pleasure to get him to talk about the 'twenties. He will discuss rugby football, ancient and modern, quite readily and with authority, but never talk about himself as a player. His criticism of the modern game can be harsh and severe, and his comments upon bad play are often ruthless.

Having achieved everything in the game as a player and administrator, he is a shrewd observer. Having succeeded in business, he is well able to travel, and has travelled to watch the game in many countries, as well as discussing it with officials, often into the early hours of the morning. In discussion he can cause one to get annoyed, but the answer is always to stay as cool and unrelenting as Waddell, for he appreciates, more than anything, a worthy opponent!

Those who have played and served with him in the game are immensely loyal to his views. Many of the younger players look upon him as a 'dictator' of the old school—a traditionalist, an unyielding conservative, but on further acquaintance they find him deeply interested and devoted to the game, for Herbert Waddell has 'lived' rugby football since he was a small boy.

He was introduced to it at Glasgow Academy by his games master, J. C. Scott, who taught the basic principles, fitness, enthusiasm, accurate passing, low tackling, backing-up and kicking the ball. At Fettes College, during World War I, the pupils played rugby on five days of the week, and if the grounds were frozen the players went on a daily three-mile run, and six miles on Saturday if there were no match! It was this intensive coaching that produced so many fine players, and the same principles hold good today.

Waddell was three years in the 1st XV with G. P. S. Mac-

pherson, D. J. MacMyn and W. B. Scott, and all four later
played together for Scotland. After the war, Waddell joined
Glasgow Academicals and was actually chosen for an Inter-
City match while in his club's 2nd XV, and then on the following Saturday appeared in his first Scottish trial. In his first
appearance in his club's 1st XV he was at centre and playing
against Oxford University, who had Macpherson at centre.
Waddell remained at centre for his club, who had Nelson
and Dykes at half-back, but in the trials of 1923-24 he played
at outside-half for the winning Rest XV and won his first of
15 caps against France. It proved a special occasion!

Owing to heavy flooding the match had to be transferred
from Stade Colombes to Stade Pershing where the crowd
broke out on to the field of play after an 'incident' and the
referee became so worried that he did not allow Scotland to
attempt any penalty kicks at goal! Had he done so, Scotland
would have won instead of losing 10-12. Waddell's next
match was against Wales, who were beaten 35-10 with the
famous all-Oxford threequarter line operating behind
Waddell. History regards this line as one of the greatest the
game has known, comparable with the Springbok quartets of
1906 and 1912, and the Welsh line of 1905.

They were a fantastic group of players: Smith, Macpherson, Aitken and Wallace; all elusive and fast; all perfect
handlers of the ball who ran from any position, and always
set out to produce the overlap. Waddell was well served by
his forwards and scrum-half Bryce, and he got his line moving
perfectly in the manner of a classical outside-half.

However, he could kick as well and landed many a
valuable dropped goal. In 1924, Scotland beat France, Wales
and Ireland, but lost to England 19-0. This was the last
defeat by the 'Sassenachs' for three years, and 1925 proved
to be one of the greatest years in Scottish rugby history. The
selectors used 19 players, who won all four matches with 77
points for and 37 against; of the 17 tries scored, the two wings,
Smith and Wallace, collected 14. Waddell dropped two goals
and played a special part in his country's brilliant play that

year. During the summer of 1924 he toured South Africa with the British Lions and, following his adventures there, returned a more experienced and mature player.

Waddell played for Scotland through 1926 and 1927 before he was ordered to give up rugby through injury and illness, but appeared once more against Wales in 1930, whom he helped defeat by dropping a goal in the last minutes of play, only to be dropped rather unwisely afterwards. When he discusses players, he regards Danny Drysdale as the best captain he played under; Ian Smith as the best wing he has seen, and Macpherson 'the best attacking centre by a thousand miles', while J. W. Scott was one of the greatest No. 8's.

Waddell believes that possession from the end of a line-out is much better than from anywhere else, but it requires accurate throwing-in, and Wallace and Smith used to practise regularly to become experts. Waddell has a deep understanding of the game when he says, 'If a player is keen, can get fit and keep fit, and be lucky enough to play in good company, whether club or international, things are very much easier than if he is a promising player in an indifferent side.'

Since he was first capped, Waddell has given loyal support and service to the Barbarians and to him their approach to rugby has always been the best. The comradeship is important and international players from all four countries can meet, play and talk freely together for five days during Easter without the pressures of the international scene.

I have discussed rugby with him during many Easter tours and although on occasions I have attacked the Barbarians for not quite being up to standard, Waddell has defended them stoutly, and only rarely have I enjoyed the best of the discussion! He has often criticised the Welsh, but really he is fond of them, and likes to count them as his true friends in the game, for making friends and keeping them is very much a part of rugby to Herbert Waddell.

He enjoyed refereeing on retiring from the field of play and was elected to the Scottish Rugby Union after the war and became its President in 1963-64, enjoying the pleasure of seeing Whineray's All Blacks drawing with Scotland. A keen administrator, he always adhered to his beliefs and sought to protect the game at all costs. To him it will remain a game for those who want hard exercise and to meet friends, and not a game where money is a paramount feature.

If you let money in, he believes that amateurism will disappear and this is the life-blood of the game; he also feels that international matches are not the real game of rugby! You may not want to agree with him, but there is a lot of sense in what he believes, and that is why I have always enjoyed listening to him rendering his 'Napoleonic' monologues!

Perhaps one can criticise Waddell for being too conservative in his approach and for feeling that the old British ways are the best for him, but at least one cannot accuse him of refusing to see for himself. At his own expense, as an administrator, he has visited South Africa, New Zealand and Australia.

Everyone wants to win and he believes that is right, but says the game must be kept clean by really strict refereeing. I recall him once holding forth at Penarth and saying, 'Referees must be ruthless with viciousness and foul play. Those who kick people deliberately and viciously, or use short-arm, savage tackles on the neck or throat, should be savagely punished. If they were, it would not happen and the game would be the better for it.' Surely, we must all agree with him on this vital matter.

I understand, although he will not admit it because he will never discuss matters considered in committees, that it was at Waddell's suggestion that the short penalty was approved and this has helped the game considerably. However, he still prefers the 3-2-3 to the 3-4-1 scrum formation, while he regrets the disappearance of the wheel, as does Lord Wakefield. The only way to improve the line-out is to have a space between the jumpers to prevent blocking, obstruction and other nonsense.

Major T. H. Vile greeting Pierre Danos of France, when President of the WRU in 1956.

Dr. Danie Craven being greeted by the Author at Cardiff in 1963.

Left: Herbert Waddell. *Right:* T. H. C. Morrison.

Left: Captain Walter E. Rees. *Right:* W. C. 'Bill' Ramsay chatting before Wales v England match of 1969.

Like father, like son, for Gordon Waddell is equally entertaining when talking rugby; they both played at outside-half on a winning side against Wales at Cardiff which, considering the few times Scotland has won there, is a rare honour! They both admire the Welsh, and I must admit I am one of their admirers.

David Jones

It is said frequently that most successful rugby administrators devote their life to the game, and this was certainly true of David Jones, of Blaina, a life member of the WRU and its former President, International Board member, national selector, county treasurer and club secretary. A senior 'deacon' of the WRU and a former school welfare officer, he cared for his invalid wife with loving tenderness, but did not miss a committee meeting or an important match, such was his devotion and enthusiasm to rugby football.

'Our Dai' was the very backbone of rugby administration in Wales, for he was a small club man who climbed to the top, working hard as he moved upwards from post to post. He gave of his best when conditions were at their worst— through the 1920's—when clubs in Wales struggled through from season to season on the proverbial shoestring. David was then secretary of Blaina and did a noble job, earning the title of 'Dai Blaina', which endeared him to all rugby men throughout the valleys of Monmouthshire.

The 1930's brought with them slightly better times for Welsh rugby and indeed for David Jones, and in 1934 he was elected to the WRU to start a career which saw him give 36 years of service at national level. In 1936 he resigned the post as secretary of Blaina to concentrate upon the 'game at the top', and in those far off days an admission fee of 3d. was charged to watch Blaina in home matches; now it is 30s.

for a seat to watch an international match at the Arms Park!

Representing Monmouthshire on the WRU with him at the time were such notable and experienced administrators as Daniel Jones and James Jarrett, both senior 'deacons', and they together with David Jones, were the true kings of Gwent rugby. David Jones was the last of those union members who served 35 years ago to survive on the governing body, and now he too has departed from the scene.

At that time, too, David Jones left coal mining and became a school welfare officer and was actively engaged in the valleys of his beloved county until he retired in 1964. He held every office in Monmouthshire County Rugby and was a true product of his environment; hard-working, sincere, straight-talking, unwavering and a committee-man devoted to the small clubs. To David Jones all men were equal in the game.

Perhaps he enjoyed most in rugby his years as a selector from 1946 to 1966, when he helped choose the Triple Crown sides of 1950, 1952 and 1965 and the British Lions' sides of 1950, 1955 and 1959. These were the great years of post-War British rugby and David Jones travelled thousands of miles watching players in action and participating in a series of adventures. He and the late Ernie Crawford, of Ireland, had a tremendous 'battle' in the committee room while selecting the 1950 British Lions for New Zealand over the claims of Welshman Dr. Jack Matthews. Crawford thought his tackling would be too vigorous for New Zealand, but David Jones was adamant and his judgment proved correct, because Matthews was one of the heroes of the tour and christened the 'iron man' by New Zealanders. If David Jones thought he was right it would take a great deal of time and persuasion to convince him otherwise, for he was a thoughtful and stubborn selector, quick to defend the players of his own country and those deserving of selection from the less-glamorous clubs.

As a member of the International Board he attended the special meeting in New Zealand held there during the 1959

Lions' tour. After the meeting he suffered a serious heart attack, but his life was saved at Rotorua Hospital as the result of expert medical skill and devoted nursing. Mrs. Jones was flown out to New Zealand to join her husband and his life was in the balance for several days before he recovered slowly and was able to return home by sea. Lesser men would not have survived this unhappy experience, and although it was not anticipated that he would continue as a rugby administrator, on his complete recovery he became even more active and was President of the WRU in 1965-66.

David Jones served on the International Board with other wise administrators in Wilfred Faull and the late Enoch Rees, both of whom, like David Jones, life members of the Union. But his great friend among the union members was former international Ivor Jones, who was President in 1968-69. Throughout their service together they were known as the Jones 'twins' and highly respected as selectors. To them the game was the thing and they were reluctant to change the order of things too rapidly; but it could not be said that they opposed change just for the sake of it.

An elder statesman and a good friend, David Jones enjoyed nothing better than a cigarette, a glass of ale and a chat about the good old days; yet few were better informed on the modern game and administrative affairs. Men like David Jones will not be replaced easily, for rugby football was in his blood and the game cannot survive or progress without such lovable characters.

W. C. Ramsay, C.B.E.

One of the best-known figures in world rugby is the popular treasurer to the Rugby Football Union, W. C. 'Bill' Ramsay, who has given a lifetime of service to the rugby game. He has visited every country and met everyone in authority working for the game. In his Churchillian manner he is one of the game's outstanding administrators and rightly can be called the 'strong man' of British rugby. He has held every office in English rugby and, at international level, has wielded considerable influence in the corridors of rugby power. It is fitting that the RFU have decided unanimously to honour him for the second time as President in 1970-71 for Centenary Year.

I am sure they have done so because they know Bill Ramsay will make a good job of it and that he will help project the image of the Union and rugby football in the very special year. A strong personality with an expert knowledge of finance and a genuine love of rugby football, he, better than most people, has been able to guide the administrative 'revolution' which has taken place in the game in the last 20 years. His broad vision and sincere belief in the right publicity and good public relations have ensured that the game has received its just quota of praise, criticism and assistance from Press, radio and television. Bill Ramsay has never failed to 'sell' the game of rugby in every country in the world, and I can think of only one other administrator who has done as much for the game, through whistle-stop tours of duty, and he is Danie Craven, of South Africa.

A successful businessman and director of several companies, Bill Ramsay has devoted valuable time and money to the cause of rugby football. Indeed, his family have become world ambassadors in the game, for Mrs. Ramsay has entertained more visiting administrators and players than any other British rugby official's wife while son Alex, a former captain of Oxford University, is following in his father's footsteps on the Rugby Football Union and in his devotion to the game. They have derived much pleasure from rugby football, but by their service to the game they have repaid the debt fourfold and the Centenary Year will see 'Mr. Rugby' make his biggest effort in the cause of the game he loves so dearly.

He is a kindly man, never seeking to boast about himself, but only about achievements by the Rugby Football Union, the four home unions and the International Board, while his club, the Old Millhillians, is very close to his heart. Administrators, officials and players enjoy trusting him with their problems, for more often than not he is able to answer them and offer much worldly advice. Bill Ramsay is a counsellor in the game and one would call him an ambassador-at-large for rugby football. In all my travels round the world I have met many people who are grateful for his help and advice. Yet, above all else, he is a realist and seeks only to safeguard the future of rugby union football. As Hon. Treasurer of the Rugby Football Union he was one of the first to appreciate that modern rugby football at representative level is big business.

A 'progressive conservative' in the game, he is prepared to consider all suggestions for its development on the field of play and the improvement of its finances, but he is not prepared to accept anything that will lower its standards. 'The game must be protected at all times, for it is our game, the game of rugby men everywhere, and while we must progress with the times and compete with other forms of sport, we must also ensure that nothing is done to make it less enjoyable to play or merely a social entertainment. Rugby football is for rugby players and this is the basis for administration at top level. It can be helped financially in many ways, but professionalism must never be allowed to rear its ugly head, because it would remove so much of the enjoyment now being achieved by those who play it in all grades and who work for it in the schools, the clubs and the counties. We have a fine game to care for, and we owe it a duty. We must never let it down.'

Bill Ramsay was educated at Mill Hill School during World War I and was captain of the school in 1918 before becoming the secretary of the Old Millhillians a year later on leaving school and playing a big part in the re-establishment of the club. Then he served on the Middlesex County committee for a couple of seasons before going to Singapore on business and playing for the local club there for three

years, as well as being its captain. On his return to England
in 1924 he played for the Old Millhillians for eight seasons
and captained the club for seven. During this period he
appeared on 18 occasions for Middlesex as a hard-working
forward and while playing enthusiastically, worked diligently
as an administrator off the field with Middlesex and the
London Counties.

When he retired from active rugby in 1932 he became the
hon. team secretary and secretary of Middlesex and served
in this capacity until 1950. Immediately after World War II
he was elected to represent Middlesex on the RFU in 1945
and the Union's Hon. Treasurer to succeed J. R. Creasey in
1950. It was from this moment onwards that he made his
impact upon the administration of the game on a broad front
and in 1954-55 he was honoured as President of the Union.

Bill Ramsay did the job well and in 1957 started a six-year
term as an England representative on the International
Board and the Four Home Unions' committee. This gave
him the opportunity to discuss the game with representatives
from all countries, but even this was not enough to satisfy
his appetite for rugby union football and he made many
visits at his own expense to overseas rugby countries,
especially when British Lions' teams were on tour, in order
that he could compare the relative styles of play and ap-
proaches to the game, as well as studying administrative
methods.

In 1963 he received the C.B.E.; in 1965 he became an
honorary vice-President of the South African Rugby Board,
while in 1969 he was made a Chevalier of the Legion
D'Honneur. These awards were well deserved and modestly
accepted. Outside of rugby football he has engaged in public
service and is chairman of the National Council of Coal
Traders. Not so long ago he survived a serious illness and it
was difficult to restrain him from returning to his beloved
Twickenham before he was really fit again. However, as
rugby football is his life, he will continue to serve it faithfully and successfully. He, perhaps more than any other

administrator, knows what is necessary to keep it healthy, vigorous and enjoyable.

Wylie Breckenridge

There can be few more independent yet more popular 'alickadoos' in world rugby than the tall, smiling Australian, John Wylie Breckenridge, one of the great characters in the game, much beloved and respected by all who know him. Affectionately named 'Breck', he is well-known from Cape Town to Aberdeen in the north; from his native Sydney to Vancouver in the west, and right across the world they enjoy meeting him for he is, perhaps, the most entertaining of post-War International Board members.

Perhaps, I have a particular interest in him because he was a prominent player in the first international match I was privileged to watch, that between Wales and the Waratahs at the Cardiff Arms Park during the 1927-28 season, when Breck was on tour as a tall, powerful flank forward. I was impressed then by his speed and ability, his dedicated enthusiasm for the game; and youthful memories are lasting ones. The late Arnold Tancred was another of the popular and successful Waratahs, later to become the élite of Australian rugby, and the country owes a great debt of gratitude to this group of remarkable players. If they had lived in the days of the Musketeers, the motto, 'All for one and one for all', would have been most apt for their approach to the game; of the team, Wallace, Lawton, Towers, Ross, Shehan, the two Fords, Finlay, Blackwood, King, Malcolm, Tancred and Breck are names as familiar in the mouth as household words in Australian rugby, for it was these stalwarts, some of them since passed from the scene, who gave to their country full international status in the game. For this they earned the gratitude and admiration of all Australians.

Breck is a 'character' and recalls his first representative match for New South Wales (home of the Waratahs) against New Zealand in 1925, when he was 22 years of age. 'I accidentally tripped one of the most famous All Blacks of the 1924-25 side, and he came up to me and said ... "That's good play, son, but if you do it again, I'll knock your b..... head off!" This was a lesson to me and I never did it again, at least to that particular All Black.'

He played it hard and tough, but gave and accepted with a smile, as when W.C. 'Wick' Powell, the celebrated Welsh scrum-half of the late 1920's and early 1930's, got so fed up with the 'friendly' attentions of Breck as a spoiling flanker in the London v Waratahs match at Twickenham, that he went to the dressing-rooms at half-time and procured a large safety-pin. This was employed early in the second half as an 'offensive weapon' to beat off Breck by pushing it into the Waratah's posterior at a scrum. There was a howl from Breck, and the pin was dropped and lost in the mud, but the status quo was established. Wick Powell confided the story to me recently in Johannesburg, while Breck always recalls it with a smile!

Breck was born in 1903 and played soccer at school, but after leaving played his first rugby on the wing for Drummoyne Juniors. At the same time he owned and successfully raced a 16 ft. sailing skiff named 'Rose', was a member of the Suburbs Athletic Club and played first-grade tennis for several years. Like most Australian youths of his era he was an all-round sportsman, but the supreme manliness of rugby football appealed to him. It was the game he enjoyed most and he is still serving it faithfully, although nowadays he can be found on the 'greens' of Warrawee Bowling Club in Sydney during several days of the week.

By 1924 Breck was an established rugby forward and in the next year achieved his Waratah cap against the N.Z. tourists, before touring Europe and Canada in 1927-28. On the tour, of happy memory, he played in 32 of the 38 matches and, best of all, met his charming wife, Jean, while visiting

Glasgow. On returning home he became honorary treasurer of the NSW Rugby Union, which was then insolvent and held the post for 20 years before handing over to his successor, out of the red, with a healthy balance sheet! In 1929 Breck played against New Zealand in the three test series and all matches were won by Australia, 9-8, 17-9 and 15-13. His last international was against the Lions' in 1930, and once again he was on the winning side.

From 1953 to 1956 he was President of the NSW and Australian Rugby Unions and was a most successful manager of the popular 1953 Wallabies in South Africa; a team that scored a record number of 93 tries for a touring team in the Republic, but the figure was improved upon two years later by Jack Siggins's Lions with 94. The 1964 South African Board's celebration book has this to say of Breck ... 'A shrewd man who was to make many a controversial and provocative statement on tour, though he was perfectly sincere in his belief that touch and tactical kicking was something overdone by South African teams.' Breck made his team run with the ball and they did it brilliantly, while he appealed throughout his career as an International Board member for the adoption of the no-kicking to touch inside the 25 law. When it was agreed to experiment universally with this in March 1968, Breck's ambition was realised. 'At long last the other unions have seen sense,' he told me in Edinburgh after the I.B. meeting, 'and it is a great day for Australia!' As the Board confirmed it as a permanent law it will remain a living tribute to Breck's work for the game.

Now a life member of the Australian and NSW unions, he has retired from professional business as a senior partner in the well-known Sydney firm of chartered accountants, Bowes and Craig, but is still a director of eight companies in the city. Tough, durable, generous, shrewd and extremely friendly, he remains one of the outstanding personalities in the game. As straight in his talk and dealings as the proverbial gun-barrel, he is my prototype of a successful rugby leader.

Strictly amateur, he played to win because he loved the game.

Dr. Danie Craven

One either likes, admires and respects Danie Craven, or one tends rather to fear him, for he is probably the most powerful living individual in rugby union football administration. Never has the phrase 'Mr. Rugby' been more aptly applied to anyone in any country, for he is truly the spirit, the brain, the power and the very soul of the game in the Republic. Though forthright in comment, steadfast in his beliefs and conservative in outlook, Craven can be roused to ire if he feels the game in South Africa is being unfairly attacked.

Yet despite his passionate defence of South African rugby at all times, he has done more for his country outside its borders than anyone else, for he has travelled extensively and continually in the cause of the game and of his country, now sadly besieged by the sporting world in general. Like all men of substance, he is prepared to listen to all points of view and to learn from those who can offer advice.

Craven talks profusely and sensibly, but he also listens, and this attribute serves him well. As a result of a rugby injury he is slightly deaf but misses little as he cups his ear to follow the whispers of the committee room or Press conferences. His mind is alert, inquisitive and retentive, while tradition dies hard within his rugby soul—although the game at top level has few more refreshing progressives than Craven. Beneath his strong exterior is a generous heart and a sensitive personality, for he suffers from the 'slings and arrows of outrageous fortune', as he did in New Zealand in 1956 when he was virtually 'crucified' in a rugby sense by the All Blacks officials, referees and players. He has recovered now from that soul-destroying experience but deep in his heart there is a wound, marked 1956.

Craven has been President of the South African Rugby Board for 13 years and, before he took the chair, had passed through every grade and office in the game in his own country, and had toured as player, manager, and observer. No South African has studied rugby more closely and no one is better suited or equipped to guide his country's rugby affairs. Even though some of his International Board colleagues from the six other member countries may accuse him of sometimes being 'too serious' or 'too technical', they have never doubted his honesty or his loyalty. Visiting pressmen have 'sniped' frequently at Craven and often disturbed his equilibrium, causing him to rush quickly to the defence of players, referees and colleagues on the S.A. Board. Often, in his case, it is his amazing loyalty to his friends that prompts the occasional outburst, but sad to say, not all his friends are as loyal to him. As a rugby official he has been in power a long time for a comparatively young man, as he is not yet sixty and is the longest serving of post-War Union Presidents.

Maxwell Price, in his enjoyable book *The Springboks Talk*, relates how Craven started playing when he was 12 years of age and later when a student at one of the world's outstanding rugby colleges, Stellenbosch, he came under the watchful eye of A. F. Markotter, who spotted him in practice and forecast he would become a Springbok. Craven was then 18 years of age and became a member of the Springbok side at 20 during the 1931-32 tour in the British Isles. He was to captain his country in 1938 and after World War II, in which he served, he was to become the 'father confessor' of Springbok rugby and a worthy successor to 'Oubaas' Markotter. Craven was born the son of a Free State farmer, and his grandfather was the son of a Yorkshire mill-owner who set off for South Africa to seek his fortune. The combination of South African durability and Yorkshire determination gave him the desire to succeed and the will to overcome problems and criticisms.

He played 16 times for South Africa between 1931 and 1938 and was captain in the exciting three-test series against Sam Walker's British Lions. After the War, Craven became a selector and joined the staff of Stellenbosch University, where he is now the head of the physical education department. Prior to the War he was on the staff of St. Andrew's College, Grahamstown, and during the War was director of Army physical training.

As a player he was a strong scrum-half with much more than a long, accurate dive pass. He was an all-round performer and a shrewd tactician, who developed ploys with his back-row forwards and, especially, the number eight forward close to the scrum. His international partners were the illustrious Bennie Osler, who was the Springbok king in his position from 1924 to 1933, and Tony Harris the brilliant runner but, in between these two fine players, Craven played twice himself in outside-half position, with the man he had superseded at scrum-half, Pierre de Villiers, playing as his partner! In South African rugby, Craven was the first of the big scrum-halves, for the selectors had always preferred the dapper brilliance of men like de Villiers, who played eight times for his country. Had overseas tours, long and short, been as frequent between the two World Wars as they have been since, then both players could have made well over twenty appearances apiece. Their style and approach differed considerably, but they were equally effective.

Craven received his international 'baptism' against Wales in 1931 'and I have scars to prove it', he told me. When he returned to Wales in 1951, he sought out all his old opponents and chatted to them, for his admiration of Welsh rugby is warm, as he believes it has much akin to that of South Africa. 'There have been few harder than the 1931 Welsh pack,' he says, 'and on a dry day their backs would have been dangerous. We had to play hard to win.' Again, South Africa did have to play hard to beat Wales in 1951, and it was this victory that gave him the greatest satisfaction on that tour.

As a selector, coach and assistant manager, he was stern and conservative in approach, yet his understanding of his players was deep and warm. He expected loyalty from them and in return gave advice, encouragement and protection and, most important perhaps, a confidence in themselves. He did not suffer 'playboys' lightly and when managing the 1956 Springboks side in Australia and New Zealand, he took rather too much upon himself. For him it was a crusade for good rugby, as he wanted the Springboks to play as they did against the 1955 Lions in a brilliant, even, series. The All Blacks wanted to win at all costs and Craven was 'crucified' in a rugby sense. It took him some time to get over the disappointment of defeat and the unyielding New Zealand approach, but he has mellowed now and, like many administrators of other countries, realises that few if any sides will lift a series again in New Zealand.

As President of the South African Board he has attended all International Board meetings of the last 12 years, and has made his presence felt in a sincere but kindly manner. He staged a brilliant 75th S.A. Board Anniversary in 1964 and helped to simplify the laws of the game in 1968-69. There is much that this flat-nosed, bright-eyed, broad-shouldered, rugby genius has done for the game and its players during his lifetime.

He still wants people to run with the ball; that advantage be given to the attacker; that the scoring awards be altered to increase the value of the try; that the differential penalty be made law, and that referees have an easier task. If he will support neutral referees in the Southern Hemisphere, then he will be able to say when he retires, if he ever does, that no one has served the game better or more faithfully without seeking any reward. He lives in Stellenbosch, a lovely sun-drenched town with more rugby fields per square mile than any other place in the world. It is the home of South African rugby and the home of Daniel Hartman Craven, the first professor of modern rugby. Those who try to follow him will not find it an easy task.

T. H. C. Morrison

His white hair belies his youthful zest for rugby football; an enthusiasm that has remained with him all his life, ever since he was born in the North Island seaside town of Gisborne in 1913. Tom Morrison, O.B.E., tall, dignified and smiling, is an ambassador for the game and has given a great deal of his leisure time to it, at home and abroad. New Zealand owes him a big debt of gratitude. He is their administrative knight in shining armour; a staunch defender of the faith, and an All Black through and through, ready to sit up all night pleading the cause of his country.

The New Zealand Rugby Union members always dress in black for formal occasions and this can be rather depressing; only the members with warm personalities and a sense of humour can burst through this rather funereal façade which gives New Zealand rugby an atmosphere of grim seriousness. Tom Morrison bursts through the 'uniform' like a happy lay-preacher, for beneath the dark suiting beats a warm heart and a puckish sense of humour.

When he laughs, it is with an infectious giggle; he much enjoys a practical joke, and he is quick to spot the idiosyncrasies of others across the conference table. Often he has commented amusingly upon personalities in the game, and with a twinkle in his eye he has gently led many an 'opponent' along the wrong path before revealing the real point of the discussion. However, he is a great 'peace-maker' and pours oil on troubled waters with considerable ease and grace.

I remember him in 1966, dashing from dressing-room to dressing-room at Eden Park, Auckland, following the rugged, blow-by-blow, Auckland v Lions match. He told both captains of the day what he thought about the display and issued a 'damping-down' statement to the Press. Morrison is the equivalent of the American oil industry's 'hell-fighter'

46

and is expert at subduing controversy. In this respect New Zealand owes him much, for he has saved them from much adverse criticism—not all of it undeserved. Morrison is a rugby diplomat, a wise counsellor, shrewd and generous, but unyielding if he believes he is right!

When he and Jack Griffiths were in harness at International Board meetings, they were a real pair of jokers. In their special way, they conceded nothing, but did it so nicely that everyone felt they had conceded something. In fact, they were so professional in their approach and so knowledgeable about the game that they were always more than one jump ahead of their rivals.

In discussion one does not always agree with Morrison, but he will agree to disagree gently, and I can imagine myself discussing the pros and cons of neutral referees with him until the end of time. Again, he will defend All Blacks forward tactics, and although a former threequarter, he does not want to see power taken from the forwards because that is the real strength of New Zealand rugby. He did not agree to the inclusion of the Australian touch-line 'dispensation' as permanent law, but New Zealanders have now done so and they are wise.

A modest man; a good family man; one proud of his country and keen enough to fight for it, and for all rugby players and free men, in the heat of North Africa and the rains of Italy during World War II.

In 1925, when he was 12 years of age, his family moved from Gisborne to Timaru, which is a big move in New Zealand—from the North Island to the South, but Timaru's Boys High School has a reputation in sport second to none. Morrison loved games and excelled as a youth at rugby football, athletics and tennis. At the age of 17 he appeared for South Canterbury on the wing. By the time he was 21 he was in the South Island side and an All Black reserve for the Springbok test series during the 1937 tour. Had he not been injured he would have played in the Second Test.

In 1938 he became an All Black—an important ambition

realised for this happy footballer—with a tour of Australia under the captaincy of N. A. 'Brushy' Mitchell and appeared in all three tests. At this time he stood six feet and weighed 12 st. 7 lb., which was ideal for a fast-moving wing. In the side were many players who remained close friends of his—in particular, Jack Griffiths and Charles Saxton. All the matches were won, including the three tests, and Tom enjoys recalling that Jack Griffiths met his charming wife, Jean, on the tour and that their two families have remained close friends, but I know that Jack and Tom receive a great deal of 'stick' from Mrs. Griffiths on rugby matters!

The next tour for Morrison would have been to South Africa in 1940 but that was cancelled owing to the War and in that year he found himself in Egypt with the N.Z. forces. He played much rugby there and eventually returned home as Captain Morrison in 1944, to play rugby again in Wellington where he became immensely popular. In 1947 he was offered the captaincy of New Zealand at 33 years of age but refused the rare honour, believing that he was too old for the job and, instead, allowed himself to be voted on to the Executive of the NZRU.

Actually, he was only the sixth All Black to join the governing body, following Harry Paton, Billy Wallace, Alexander Macdonald, Jim Parker and Frank Kilby, and his election when an active player was something unheard of in his country. Later he became a selector and was the convenor of selectors during the memorable 1956 tour of New Zealand by the Springboks. They were hectic days, some of which are best forgotten, and the next step up the rugby ladder for Morrison was the Chairmanship of the NZRU, before the final accolade of being elected a representative on the International Board, and the award of the O.B.E. I shall always think of him as the 'happy' man in black!

Jack Siggins (right) returns with the successful 1955 Lions Team
from South Africa. With him are the captain, Robin Thompson
and Assistant Manager, D. E. 'Danny' Davies.

John Gwilliam in his
first match as captain of
Wales against England at
Twickenham, 1950.

Cliff Morgan starting the movement that led to the try by Ken
Jones against Ireland at Dublin in 1952.

J. A. E. Siggins

Genial Jack Siggins is a big man, not perhaps as big a man, physically, now as when he captained Ireland with such skill and enthusiasm before World War II, but a big rugby man. He has served it well, as a player and administrator, and still enjoys the proud record of being the most successful Lions' manager to leave these shores this century. He has retired from most of his international administrative duties, but he is still loyal to his first love, the Ulster Union, and acts as one of their most-experienced elder statesmen, although still a young man at the age of 60!

You have to travel and live with a man, to suffer success and defeat, in peace or war, to really know him, and during four months with the Lions in South Africa in 1955 I got to know Jack Siggins. A friendship was started that I much enjoy still even though we meet no more than once or twice a year, because we were both fortunate in that we saw some outstanding rugby and shared life with a party of remarkable young men. There were 31 players, two managers and two (later three) pressmen on this colourful trip and there cannot have been a happier one.

Jack Siggins was the honorary manager and although he admits, 'I was indeed fortunate to have such a wonderful group of players to command', it was his integrity, warm charm, dignity and ability to give the players just enough freedom, and no more, to develop their individual flair that ensured success. His considerable knowledge and experience of big rugby always stood him in good stead and, even in the few moments of stress on the tour, he remained outwardly calm. Occasionally, in the privacy of his hotel room, he gave vent to his feelings and he was not reluctant to put an erring player in his place during team meetings.

Jack has always held firm views upon the game and would

49

change them only if he thought it would really benefit all concerned. Never one to put his head into the sand and listen to no one, he did so, especially in public, but rarely was drawn into public or Press controversy. For him the dignity of the game was all-important and South Africa came to respect him and admire his team. The Lions of 1955 proved themselves the most popular ever to visit the Republic and while much of the popularity was achieved by their own skill, speed and personality, some of the credit must surely go to Jack Siggins, a shrewd manager who had the ability, good humour and, indeed, patience, to set an excellent example to his young charges.

Jack was born in 1909 and educated at Armagh Royal School and the Methodist College, Belfast, and at 18 years of age made the transfer from school to senior football, playing for Ulster against the 1927-28 touring Wallabies. Four years later he achieved his ambition by making the first of 24 consecutive appearances for Ireland; a considerable achievement. This was in 1931 and after a career of consistent service as a forward, pack leader and captain, he retired in 1937. Through three seasons, 1934-36, he was the Irish leader and remembers, especially, the day at Cardiff in March 1936 when the penalty goal by Vivian Jenkins gave Wales victory and the Championship while robbing Ireland of the Triple Crown!

Jack's club was the Collegians, former pupils of Methodist College, and he captained them for many years, as well as being a regular member of the Barbarians. He started serving the Ulster Branch of the Irish Rugby Union in 1932 and has now completed 38 years of uninterrupted devotion to Ulster rugby. He became a selector for Ireland after the War and shared in the Triple Crown triumphs of 1948 and 1949. The managership of the Lions' side followed in 1955, and the Presidency of the Irish Union in 1962-63, while he served for 11 years as a member of the International Board from 1957 to 1968.

During this period of important service to the game's

highest authority Jack Siggins visited Australia, New Zealand, Canada and South Africa and proved a knowledgeable diplomat. Yet he maintained his strong views on the game and how it should be played and administered. From good Ulster stock, he is a Protestant, a Unionist, and a monarchist, and he served as an officer in the Army during hostilities from 1940-46. A good family man, he is an excellent shot, a fine fisherman and a championship golfer, although he says, 'This is now beyond my fitness!'

Professionally, he was in insurance from 1927 until retiring in 1968. Many who do not know Jack have thought him a little 'stuffy', but this is far from the real person, for he has a keen sense of humour, an infectious chuckle and a deep understanding of people. He expects loyalty in his friends and is not given to publicity or sensationalism in the game. He has a code for rugby football, on and off the field, and as 'Number One' I got to know him well, for the best way to know any man is to eat pineapple with him at breakfast while the 'Press' are getting at his team (and himself) for not being fit!

His team talk before the memorable First Test of 1955 at Ellis Park was simply ... 'This is it chaps ... this is D Day ... go to it ... do your best and play rugby ... you can win!' They did win, and Jack bought the team beer. When they lost the Second Test at Cape Town, he bought them champagne, and didn't talk about the defeat until Monday. For my money he was a successful manager.

V. E. Kirwan

The man behind the scenes at International Board level is the Board's honorary secretary, V. E. 'Eddie' Kirwan, a likeable but unobtrusive personality, who hovers in the background at official functions, remains the 15th member of the Board, and sign the official statement after each meeting.

Well-known in Ireland he is, perhaps, unknown by rugby followers in other countries, but respected and admired by administrators everywhere.

Short, dapper and dignified in appearance, Eddie Kirwan has a delightful Irish brogue which is captivating in conversation, and an extremely pleasant manner, although he has to walk diplomatically through the rugby corridors of power and never utter a word out of place because he carries so many important secrets! He is one of Ireland's senior solicitors and head of the firm he founded and which enjoys an extensive practice in Dublin.

Before he was invited to become the secretary of the International Board, to succeed Harry Thrift in 1956, Kirwan had given a career of devoted service to the game in Ireland and had played an important part in the development of the Irish Rugby Union, of which he was President in 1952-53. Like all Irish administrators, he is intensely amateur-conscious in his approach and is a 'defender of the rugby faith' in every sense of the phrase. Eddie Kirwan does not tolerate fools in the game gladly and is outspoken in his private comment during friendly discussions.

Born in Dublin, Kirwan was educated at Mountjoy School and Trinity College, where he won a silver medal in his solicitors' final examination. He played his rugby for the Palmerston Club, which he joined in 1920, appearing for them at full back for 11 consecutive seasons, and was unlucky during his best years not to achieve international honours because of the long and successful reign by W.E. Crawford in the position.

As is customary in many senior Irish clubs, he was a member of the Palmerston Club committee while playing, and following the captaincy for two seasons he later became President of the club. After World War II he became the President of the Leinster branch and in 1948 was elected a member of the IRFU's committee. Proving a most energetic and popular member of the union's executive, he was honoured as its President in 1952-53 and, finally, elected unanimously as hon. secretary of the International Board in 1956, which he has served loyally and effectively ever since. Indeed, it will be difficult to succeed such an industrious administrator!

While a senior member of the Irish Union's executive, he did a tremendous amount of work in the conversion of the Lansdowne Road ground in Dublin and the erection of its new double-decker stand. The project has proved of immense financial benefit to Irish rugby after a period of six years, during which the various hurdles were surmounted, including that of acquiring financial support, and much of the credit is due to the determination and diplomacy of Eddie Kirwan.

During his term as Secretary of the International Board he has travelled widely, studying the game, for in 1952 he was in the Argentine with the Irish team, followed by International Board meetings in New Zealand in 1959 and South Africa in 1964. These trips provided him with the opportunity of visiting Australia and Rhodesia and he quickly made friends in these countries, while ready to discuss world rugby with the various administrators he met.

His enthusiasm for rugby is considerable, but like most Irishmen he has many other sporting interests, being a keen yachtsman and a better-than-average golfer. During the summer he can often be seen at the Royal St. George Yacht Club in Dun Laoghaire, of which club he is a trustee. On first meeting him, and not knowing of his legal and rugby background, one would assume quite easily that he was a deep-sea sailor, with his tanned complexion and keen eye!

However, rugby remains his first love and he devotes almost all his leisure time to the game, as one would expect from a man who comes from a rugby family. Kirwan is one of four brothers who played for the Palmerston Club and three of them at the same time for the first fifteen. Rugby in Ireland is based upon the support of families like his and the dapper little Irishman has done much for the game in his own country. While many would wish him to promulgate more readily, details of the work of the International Board, it should be remembered that at all times he is sworn to secrecy. Indeed, Eddie Kirwan is the most important 'backroom boy' in the game, but he cannot change the present system of voting in the constitution of the International Board—it is a task for the seven member countries to consider!

Brig. H. L. G. Hughes

One of the best known and most popular of rugby 'alickadoos' is the President of the Barbarians Club, who has given a lifetime of service to the game and who believes that, at all times, rugby football must be played for enjoyment, whether it be a school cup game or an overseas test match. Born in the small town of Ventersburg, in the Orange Free State, at the end of the last century of a Welsh father and mother who was half-Welsh Brigadier Glyn Hughes could justifiably call himself a true Welshman, but he prefers to call himself a rugby man because the game to him is international. His club, the Barbarians, is known throughout the world and respected for its approach, its beliefs and its desire to produce all that is best in the game on the field of play and all that is truly sporting off it.

'Hughie' of the Barbarians is the Club's father figure and follows in line a short but honoured list of senior 'alickadoos' of the club, W. P. Carpmael, who founded the Barbarians in 1890, Emile de Lissa, and H. A. Haigh Smith. He is the dynamic centre of the club's activities. Behind his charming manner and casual air is hidden a clear brain and an amazing knowledge of the game and its players. His brilliant record in two World Wars and his medical experience enables him to judge men fairly and accurately, and very few players who enter the sacred confines of the Barbarians' Club are not good fellows. Occasionally, an outstanding player may miss the honour of being invited to play for the Barbarians, and this is sad, because even Hughie and his committee can make an occasional mistake. Yet, such errors, if they be so, can be counted on the fingers of one hand down through the 80 years of the club's existence!

When Hughie was two years of age his father died, and he returned with his mother to Britain and for five years attended a preparatory school at Newport, where he was coached in rugby football by one of the 'select few', C. M. Pritchard, of Newport, who was in the historic Welsh XV that defeated New Zealand at Cardiff in 1905. 'Pritchard introduced me to the game and encouraged me to enjoy myself in it, and I have never forgotten his words of advice.' From Newport, Glyn Hughes went on to Epsom College, where he became captain of the first fifteen before entering medical school in London and joining the Blackheath Club. As a young club player he possessed more than average ability and was soon in the first fifteen, which contained six internationals in its pack. His first county game was for Middlesex against Somerset at Wellington and, strange to relate, his last county game 17 years later was for Devon against Somerset at Wellington!

He volunteered for active service when the Great War broke out in 1914 and won the D.S.O. as a subaltern and when promoted to captain, won a bar to the D.S.O., the M.C. and certain French decorations. On returning to civilian life he resumed his medical career and became captain of United Hospitals side in 1920, as well as playing for Exeter and Devon. His long association with the Barbarians began in 1912-13, when he made his first tour in South Wales, and he remained a playing member until 1926. On retiring from the field of play he became a junior alickadoo and then hon. treasurer of the club from 1928. Recently he confessed to me that he had missed only one Barbarian tour in South Wales since 1913 and then for professional reasons. His association with the Blackheath Club has been equally devoted and he was its President for 25 years, while now he is the hon.

treasurer of the Four Home Unions tours committee, which, as he says, is a 'busy job'.

While he has never been a member of the Rugby Football Union, Glyn Hughes has been closely associated with the development of the game in many countries and in 1936 he toured with the British Lions' in the Argentine as an official referee for the matches and hon. medical officer. Since the war he has managed the Barbarians on their three overseas tours, to Canada and twice to South Africa, and made a lasting impression with his hosts for his remarkable sportsmanship, his personal modesty, and his unassuming efficiency in the role of a senior tourist and hon. manager.

Because of his outstanding ability and warm personality he is able to win easily the respect of his fellow alickadoos and the players in his side and, while he practises in management the 'iron hand in the velvet glove', he is always unobtrusive in his approach to problems and people. Perhaps the several horrifying experiences of the war-time years have imbued him with greater compassion than that possessed by most men and, as the first senior Allied officer to enter the dreaded Belsen Camp at the close of the European War, he has a genuine hate for evil and wrong doing.

To talk to him about rugby football is always a fascinating event whenever he comes to South Wales. Last Easter we discussed modern rugby in detail and it was interesting to hear him analyse the game as he played it and as it is played now. With due deference to the fine players of today, he felt that rugby football, as a whole, was not all that faster, though in certain positions there had been a speeding-up in approach. Glyn Hughes played all his rugby in the front row as a prop or a hooker, and he started in the era of 'first up, first down' and ended his career in an era dominated by the specialisation as brilliantly developed by Wavel Wakefield. Many are the famous players he played with and against, as well as inviting to become Barbarians, but he regards the greatest ever to wear the black and white jersey of his club, as Charles Pillman of Blackheath, England and the British Lions.

Last winter the Barbarians won all four matches in Wales and won them well by playing good rugby and this pleased the Club's President, for he would prefer to lose a match playing good rugby than to win at all costs. He is anxious not to 'professionalise' the game by taking up too much of the players' time although often he is prepared to compromise. For instance he allowed the Barbarians to have a 'coaching squad' session on the Friday before the Springboks match at Twickenham, and although the Barbarians are always a 'scratch' side their blending is due to their spirit of approach. They feel that good rugby players, with the right ideas, can always play together and judging by their record over eighty years, the Barbarians have been most successful.

Many young players have been groomed for stardom and caught the eyes of national selectors while playing with more experienced players in the ranks of the Barbarians, and there can be no better example of this than the case of the fine England wing, Hal Sever, who 'graduated' in South Wales. Again, Glyn Hughes presides over the Barbarians at their Welsh headquarters at the Esplanade Hotel, Penarth each Easter, like a rugby 'father-confessor', and the young players learn much in open discussion with such rugby wise alicka-doos as Herbert Waddell and Jock Wemyss. How many table cloths have been stained by hurried plans of rugby fields and specialised movements is difficult to assess, but much has been learned by many at the famous Hotel.

On one famous occasion the Barbarians moved away slightly from their tactical approach and that was in 1961 at Cardiff, when they inflicted the only defeat of their tour upon Avril Malan's fifth Springboks. The tourists were unbeaten before the match and had suggested that, rather than play a 'straight' match the two teams should combine but the Barbarians did not approve of this suggestion because to them the losing of a record was not all that important. The match was won by a magnificent forward display on the part of the Barbarians and the captured Springbok head now has a place of honour in Penarth. It was a special day remem-

bered by all Welshmen and did much to further the close
relations between the Barbarians and Wales. Even Glyn
Hughes was delighted to receive the 'head' from the tourists!

PART TWO

The Matches

Twelve Unforgettables

Cardiff v Australia, 1947

Cardiff Arms Park, September 27, 1947

The first official tour after the Second World War was that made by the Third Wallabies from Australia under the managership of former Waratah Arnold Tancred and the captaincy of W. M. 'Bill' McLean. They produced quite a remarkable record in a lively and, occasionally, controversial tour while stimulating the game considerably in the British Isles. In all they played 35 matches in Europe, won 29 of them and lost six, with 500 points scored for and 243 against. They lost two of their five international matches, to Wales and France; and were defeated by Cardiff, Combined Lancashire and Cheshire, the London Counties, and the Barbarians, in the other matches.

This is a record few Australian sides have improved upon; although the 1927-28 Waratahs lost one less match they were defeated by England and Scotland in International matches. The Third Wallabies arrived in this country fit and healthy, having enjoyed the good food and sun of Australia for a couple of years after the end of the War, although many of them had served in the forces and one had been a P.O.W. of the Japanese. Compared with most rugby teams of the era, they were bounding with energy and eager to play hard in the traditional, confident Australian manner, and their early matches encouraged this approach.

They beat Devon and Cornwall Combined 17-7, the Midland Counties 22-14, Somerset and Gloucester 30-8 and Abertillery and Cross Keys Combined 6-3, before they reached Cardiff for the fifth match of the tour. Cardiff had just started their most successful post-War season, so the clash of two such sides was certain to create something of a sensation—and it did!

As for many touring teams, before and after the Third Wallabies, the Cardiff Arms Park was not a lucky ground. Tancred's men were soundly defeated by a goal, a penalty and a try (11) to a penalty (3) and found the experienced Cardiff side, led by the 'master' at scrum-half Haydn Tanner, stronger physically than they were and a better combination. The Australian 'fire' was quelled by solid scrummaging, good line-out work and devastating tackling, and it took the tourists some time to recover from the experience. Recover they did, even though they suffered the loss of their captain, McLean, with a broken leg in the very next match at Twickenham, and finished the tour by sharing in one of the most exciting and delightful matches ever played by the Barbarians in Wales.

Towards the end of the tour, in order to raise funds to send the Wallabies home via Canada, where they played a couple of matches, the Four Home Unions with the help of the WRU, the Cardiff Club and the Barbarians, staged a special match between the Wallabies and the Barbarians at the Arms Park. The match was a considerable success and each touring team visiting the British Isles since that date has played the Barbarians, almost always at Cardiff.

The Wallabies lacked genius at outside-half, although the players in the position were sound enough, and this slight weakness robbed them of possible greatness. They had a determined, mobile pack of forwards, and one of the best group of covering back-row forwards I have seen, with A. J. Buchan, an outstanding number eight. The loss of McLean was considerable on the flank, but Windon and Keller (who was later to play for Scotland) did extremely well. Burke was a player of promise at scrum-half and became one of the best in the position with world-class rating. At threequarter, young Allan in the centre took over the captaincy when McLean was injured and performed admirably, while Eastes and Tonkin plus McBride were wings of quality. Eastes was a remarkable player, who suffered a serious arm injury in the twelfth match of the tour at Newport. All trained keenly and were extremely fit.

During their first week in Wales the Wallabies trained hard, were fêted and attended many functions, while Cardiff also prepared well under Tanner, who had brilliant midfield players like Williams, Matthews and Cleaver to help him; an experienced full-back in Trott and forwards of skill in James, Davies, Tamplin, Manfield and Evans, all of whom were to be capped for Wales during the season, when the Club supplied as many as eleven internationals, a world record.

A crowd of 44,000 spectators, the largest crowd at a club match since the restart after the War, sang the anthems beautifully and play started in good conditions. Eastes, with a long devastating run that took him past defenders like a hopping kangaroo, disturbed Cardiff early on and almost brought a score, and it was unfortunate that mid-way through the first-half the Wallabies lost their hooker, Dawson, with a torn rib muscle. They played with seven forwards for the rest of the match, and as the struggle grew harder the physical contact increased in the tackles without becoming dirty.

Nick Shehadie, a popular tight forward, suffered a damaged shoulder and moved to the side of the scrum, leaving the Wallabies with 13 fit men. Cardiff held out strongly though they, too, suffered muscle damage in the bruising tackles, and especially the crash-tackling Matthews. Second-row forward Tamplin, their pack leader, gave Cardiff the lead after 20 minutes when he kicked a penalty goal. It was three-nil at the interval but, after 15 minutes of the second half, Williams cross-kicked from the left and Manfield gathered before sending D. H. Jones over at the right corner with a long pass.

Immediately afterwards, Allan reduced the lead with a magnificent penalty kick from just inside his own half, straight down field with the ball just clearing the cross bar.

Play was still keen and both sides preferred to spoil and tackle and continue the battle of physical strength, and it was only near the end that the depleted Wallabies yielded another try.

Manfield and Roberts made ground at forward during strong pressure by Cardiff, and Davies (as popular a figure as any on the field) got a fine try with a final burst of speed. Tamplin kicked a magnificent goal off the touch-line and the match was over.

It was one of the hardest, clean, touring team versus club matches I have seen in any country and the mounting list of injuries, as play proceeded, suggested that it would end with even less than a dozen players a side! The Wallabies suffered considerably from the loss of hooker Dawson, but Cardiff were the better side on the day. In hard and fast going on a firm surface the Wallabies chose to make it a stern forward contest with plenty of movement so that their weight momentum and fitness would reduce their opponents' stamina and speed. Cardiff, adopting the same approach, were slightly the cleverer and the stronger, and better served in mid-field.

It was a remarkable tribute to both sides that tempers did not become frayed in the tense vigour of the match, but it was an affair of honour, as to which pack of forwards were the fittest and strongest. Had not Dawson and Shehadie been injured in the first half, it would have been a much closer affair, of course, and had Eastes got a try early in the match when he looked so magnificent, running down the touch-line, then things would have been more even.

It was an heroic struggle and the Cardiff 'veterans' lasted well, but when I visited the dressing-rooms afterwards they looked like war-time casualty clearing stations, and all thirty players knew they had been in a match of some consequence. Referee Goldsworthy did well, but the spirit of the sides contributed much to a fascinating study in the physical side of hard, honest, purposeful rugby. It has never been a game for weaklings, but this one was rare and when Tanner was carried from the field, shoulder high, one felt that he had led a side developed in war-time Britain that had more than held its own with some of the finest sons of the Commonwealth.

The Teams

Cardiff: R. F. Trott; D. H. Jones, B. L. Williams, Dr. J. Matthews, L. Williams; W. B. Cleaver, H. Tanner (capt); C. Davies, M. James, W. G. Jones, R. Roberts, W. E. Tamplin, E. Jones, L. Manfield, G. Evans.

Australians: C. J. Windsor; J. W. T. McBride, M. L. Howell, T. Allan, C. C. Eastes; N. Emery, R. M. Cawsey; R. E. McMaster, W. L. Dawson, E. Tweedale, N. Shehadie, G. M. Cooke, C. J. Windon, A. J. Buchan, W. M. McLean (captain).

Referee: G. Goldsworthy (Penarth).

England v Wales, 1950

Twickenham, January 21, 1950

Seventeen years is long enough for any country to have to wait between victories at Twickenham and this was the experience of Wales after their first victory at the ground in 1933. Yet, on January 21, 1950 they did not start the match as favourites, although finishing it in a blaze of glory. They had suffered the unhappiness of the Wooden Spoon at the end of the previous season and several outstanding players had disappeared from the scene. The Welsh fifteen contained six new caps and a new captain. Yet history was about to repeat itself.

Watcyn Thomas was appointed Captain in 1933 at Twickenham to lead Wales for the first time and it was his driving force, plus good team work, that produced the first elusive victory.

In 1950, John Gwilliam was given the leadership for the first time in his notable career as, not many hours before the kick-off, the appointed captain, Bleddyn Williams, had been forced to withdraw through illness and injury. The senior forward at the time, Rees Stephens, had been forced to withdraw earlier through injury, and his absence enabled Roy John, also of Neath, to set out on a colourful career in the game in the second-row.

England included several new caps, and three of the team were overseas players, having qualified for England by residence at Oxford University. This was the normal procedure at the time, but there followed later a gentleman's agreement between the Home Countries in which players could nominate the country they wished to play for but, after so doing, were not eligible for other countries. Rugby football has no strict qualification law as in the Association code, and the reason why is that there is greater migration from country to country by rugby players.

Unfortunately for England, the lively back-row forward D. B. Vaughan of the Royal Navy and Headingley, who was later to manage the 1962 Lions, pulled a muscle after 10 minutes' play and this weakened the England pack. Before the match there were unprecedented scenes outside the ground and the RFU secretary, Col. Douglas Prentice, following consultation with the police, decided to close down the turnstiles at 1.30 p.m., an hour before the kick-off, leaving open only those gates for stand ticket holders. Locked outside were 20,000 supporters who had travelled up to Twickenham from Wales and they were most disappointed. Fortunately, kindly householders in the Twickenham area, in possession of television sets, opened their doors to the disappointed supporters, many of whom saw the match 'on the box' while watching television for the first time in their lives, as the Wenvoe and St. Hillary transmitters had not been constructed at the time.

The 74,000 spectators inside and the many thousands outside saw an exciting match that produced a memorable victory for Wales. The play was full of incident, from first whistle to last, and the foundation of the Welsh success was laid by the fine work of the Welsh forwards. Again, the Welsh team was a match-winning force, united in purpose and in the execution of its tactics, and the man who blended and disciplined the side was the new captain, John Gwilliam. Calm and deliberate, he inspired his men by personal example and intelligent direction. In the set scrums, at the line-out, and in the loose he drove them hard and they produced the necessary fire and vigour, plus expertise, to win enough possession for a back division that improved rapidly after the opening 10 minutes of play. Gwilliam contributed much to the settling-down period by making several marks, often when not under pressure, in order to slow down the tempo of the play and enable his younger players, appearing at the ground for the first time, to get accustomed to the international atmosphere.

The Welsh front row of C. Davies, D. M. Davies and J. D. Robins settled into a compact unit and at the line-out John, Gwilliam and Hayward as a jumping combination were most impressive. Don Hayward was the strong man of the Welsh pack, as he was to be for the British Lions in New Zealand a few months later. W. R. Cale and R. T. Evans were outstanding back-row forwards and it was their tremendous spoiling that curbed the England halves. Behind them W. R. Willis, playing his first international, was sound at scrum-half and W. B. Cleaver at outside-half, who always played with confidence in every match, shrewdly directed the general tactics.

The threequarter line, with J. Matthews as the strong man, and K. J. Jones as its speed merchant, probed and harassed, not so much as a unit but as individuals, and Matthews's tackling was often devastating. A new young star to burst into the international firmament was full-back Lewis Jones from Devonport Services who, at 18 years nine months, became the second youngest player to appear for Wales and he performed with the confidence of a veteran. His fielding, positioning and kicking were splendid and his eagerness to launch attacks highlighted a 'new look' in the Welsh approach and laid the foundations of a spectacular career in the union game for this young West Walian before he became an illustrious name in the Rugby League code. On this special day the Twickenham crowd gave him the accolade of success that only few enjoy in their first international match.

England had to play under difficulties as a result of the early injury to Vaughan, but until Wales settled down they had slightly the better of the play. L. B. Cannell was a centre of quality with J. V. Smith always a fast elusive wing. Had these backs received better and more frequent possession, it would have been much harder for Wales to contain them, and thus it was the work of the Welsh forwards in denying England possession that enabled Wales, eventually, to take control and go on to win. Yet England never gave up fighting to maintain the tension and excitement of a sporting contest.

It was England who took the lead after 10 minutes play when the clever Smith moved inside to intercept a pass from M. C. Thomas to T. J. Brewer, on the left wing, when the Welsh backs were handling inside their own half. Accelerating, Smith raced away to the corner flag ahead of the covering defence and he drew Lewis Jones across ahead of him before moving slightly outwards for the corner flag. Jones dived, but just missed his tackle on Smith, who scored a real wing's try. M. B. Hofmeyr converted beautifully from the touch-line and for a moment Wales, five points in arrears, believed the Twickenham 'bogy' to be as effective as ever!

However, they had forgotten the potential of Lewis Jones. He fielded the ball just inside the England half and, instead of kicking back over his forwards to touch in the orthodox manner, he set sail, running diagonally across the field. When approaching the left touch-line he straightened up to outwit the England mid-field backs and then with a delightful swerve, set off once more towards the right-hand touch-line, before handing on to M. C. Thomas, up in support. Wing forward R. T. Evans was with Thomas and he sent Cliff

Davies diving over the line for a memorable try. Robins did not convert and it was 5-3 at the interval, although J. V. Smith went near to scoring a second try for England.

In the second half Lewis Jones placed a good penalty goal when England infringed at a line-out to put Wales in the lead. Immediately they scored again, to consolidate their position. Cleaver short-punted diagonally from outside the England '25' and as Boobbyer gathered he was crash-tackled by Matthews. The ball went loose and Cleaver tapped it gently over the England goal-line for Cale to get the try and Lewis Jones convert. It was too late for England to regain the lead and, try as they did, they could not disturb the growing confidence of the Welshmen, and the match ended with supporters swarming on to the field, to celebrate an eleven points to five victory.

They hoisted Lewis Jones and John Gwilliam to their shoulders and marched them away with pride to the dressing-room. For Wales it was a special moment of triumph and laid low the Twickenham bogy, a 'killing' that was long overdue!

The Teams
England: M. B. Hofmeyr (Oxford Univ.); I. J. Botting (Oxford Univ.), L. B. Cannell (Oxford Univ.), B. Boobbyer (Oxford Univ.), J. V. Smith (Cambridge Univ.); I. Preece (Coventry) capt., G. Rimmer (Waterloo); J. McG. Kendall-Carpenter (Oxford Univ.), E. Evans (Sale), W. A. Holmes (Nuneaten), G. R. d'A Hosking (Devonport Ser.), H. A. Jones (Barnstable), H. D. Small (Oxford Univ.), D. B. Vaughan (Headingley), J. J. Cain (Waterloo).

Wales: B. L. Jones (Devonport Ser.); K. J. Jones (Newport), J. Matthews (Cardiff), M. C. Thomas (Devonport Ser.), T. J. Brewer (Newport); W. B. Cleaver (Cardiff), W. R. Willis (Cardiff); J. D. Robins (Birkenhead Park), D. M. Davies (Somerset Police), C. Davies (Cardiff), R. John (Neath), D. J. Hayward (Newbridge), W. R. Cale (Pontypool), J. A.

Gwilliam (Edinburgh Wanderers, capt.), R. T. Evans (Newport).

Referee: N. H. Lambert (Ireland).

Cardiff v Newport, 1951

Cardiff Arms Park, February 17, 1951

If not the oldest, if not the greatest, then Newport and Cardiff must be the two most illustrious rugby clubs in the world, and their meeting, four times a season, still provides some of the hardest and most near to test standard of any club rugby in the world. Newport, formed in 1874, with six invincible seasons behind them, and Cardiff in 1876, were in their 75th year when these two clubs met in a very special match at the Arms Park on February 17, 1951.

Cardiff had already beaten Newport four times in a season on three occasions, but Newport had never done this to Cardiff, and still have to achieve the feat, though often getting desperately close with three victories and a draw in the fourth match. On the other hand, Cardiff had not achieved invincibility and are still without such a record. Yet in this 1950-51 season, Newport had gone 24 matches without defeat by the time this third meeting with Cardiff arrived and they were in line for another invincible year and the cherished four victories over Cardiff!

Both sides contained 1950 Lions', for Cardiff had Dr. Jack Matthews, B. L. Williams, W. R. Willis and C. Davies, and Newport two in K. J. Jones and R. T. Evans. Cardiff included 10 players who were already capped or capped later, while Newport fielded five. Thus it was no ordinary club match, but a clash of giants and the referee, Ivor David, of Neath, was another giant and possibly the best of all post-War referees. Efficient, understanding, decisive, cool and unobtrusive, he deserved his title of the ghost with a whistle!

As Newport had already beaten Cardiff 8-3 and 8-6 in the first two meetings of the season, interest in this match was fantastic and, having followed Welsh club rugby for forty years, I cannot recall any club match of my lifetime attracting so much attention, even more than the meeting of unbeaten Llanelli and Cardiff in the early 1930's. That match attracted over 30,000 to the Arms Park and in 1949-50 the Cardiff and Swansea match attracted over 35,000 to the same place. Swansea won through a thrilling second-half recovery, and as the thousands poured into the Arms Park on this February day in 1951 the omens were not good for Cardiff. There were well over 40,000 spectators when play started and the final additions carried out by hon. secretary, Brice Jenkins, were quite sensational.

The match proved to be a world record for any club game not involving a touring team, and is likely to stand for a long, long time. A total of 48,500 spectators paid £2,587 to watch it and they had better value for their money than in many an international match. If for nothing else achieved in their colourful histories, this match elevated them to the top of the popularity polls for clubs throughout the world, and set the seal upon the true strength and drawing power of Welsh club rugby in the post War world. The Welsh Rugby Union, itself, is often slow to appreciate the greatness and status of its senior clubs, and while it is democratic in treating all alike, the big clubs like Newport, Cardiff, Swansea, Llanelli, Neath, Aberavon, Bridgend and the like are deserving of special treatment and consideration. They are the shop-window of Welsh rugby and the makers of international sides.

It had rained at the Cardiff Arms Park for a few hours early on the morning of February 17, 1951 and the ground had been made heavy, although the weather was dry when Ken Jones and W. E. Tamplin led their teams on to the historic turf and the record crowd roared in greeting their heroes. Newport had Jones, Lane, Burnett, Williams, Edwards and Evans, and Cardiff a string of personalities, but as in all matches between the two clubs the sides started from scratch, for rarely are there favourites!

So it was on this day, and Cardiff had use of a strong high wind in the first half. They had the better of this period, but Newport were amazingly stubborn in defence and they yielded little for Cardiff achieved only a penalty goal. This was kicked by Tamplin after 10 minutes of play when Newport were guilty of feet-up. It was an unhappy omen for Newport, as Tamplin—their bogy man—had beaten them on many occasions and such kicking form was depressing for them, but cheering for Cardiff. Yet, strange to relate, Tamplin was not to kick another goal in this match!

For a greater part of the first half it was a forward battle and the crowd enjoyed it with the roar of encouragement rising and falling like a fierce tidal wave. No forward spared himself in either pack and while Newport had the edge in the set scrums, Cardiff were in charge at the line-out and held a slight advantage in the loose. Again, it was not a day for flowing back movements with the high wind and heavy going, but there were strong individual efforts away from the forwards and all four wings foraged and tackled like demons. Defences were defiant; each creating its own 'Verdun' for the order of the day was, and always will be in these matches, 'They shall not pass!'

Ten minutes after the interval, Newport drew level and their genuinely partisan supporters shrieked with obvious delight. Good kicking by Burnett pinned Cardiff to their own 25 and then a burst by a group of forwards from the line-out succeeded as prop Tom Sterry, a big-hearted worker, crashed over for a try. Big Ben Edwards, who scored 159 points during the season, failed with the conversion, but one felt the tension rising as well as the confidence of the Newport side.

Yet the proud and mighty Cardiff were equally determined and the heat of the struggle reached flash-point in the cauldron of rugby endeavour. It was hard and vigorous, but never dirty and the wise Ivor David—vastly experienced—

saw to it that the cauldron did not overflow into nastiness and besmirch the great occasion. This was an historic match and much was yet to happen!

Matthews, Murphy and Goodfellow were nearly over and the young Cliff Morgan, as then uncapped, wriggled and probed, but Newport, with Ackerman superb in covering defence, held out. Ten minutes from the end they got the winning try. Murphy, on the right wing for Cardiff, just failed to find touch with a clearing kick and John Lane, the Newport left wing, gathered the ball and set off up the touch-line. Always an elusive runner, he avoided tackles and coverers and got over the line to touch down behind the posts. The crowd erupted, for the stalemate had been broken while the goal kick was all too easy for Edwards.

As if this were not enough, a freak hailstorm hit the ground immediately after this score to halt proceedings for several minutes. Players lay down as the storm swept across the ground, while Jack Matthews tried to hide his broad and powerful frame behind an upright! I cannot recall such a sight before or since, not even the freak rainstorm at Canberra in 1966, when the Lions played there.

It revived Cardiff, who attacked fiercely during the remaining minutes, but they could not equalise. They almost did though, but Ken Jones got Haydn Morris with a wonderful tackle from behind. Soon the final whistle went and a very special match had ended. History had been made and both clubs added another fascinating item to their remarkable collection of records. The blue and black of Cardiff and the black and amber of Newport will continue to attract large crowds whenever they meet in fair weather or foul!

The Teams
Cardiff: R. F. Trott; D. C. Murphy, J. Matthews, B. L. Williams, H. Morris; C. I. Morgan, W. R. Willis; G. Jenkins, J. R. Phillips, C. Davies, W. E. Tamplin (capt), P. Goodfellow, J. D. Nelson, D. J. O'Brien, C. D. Williams.

Newport: R. Hughes; K. J. Jones (capt), R. D. Owen, B. Williams, J. Lane; R. Burnett, W. A. Williams; G. Hirst, L. Davies, T. Sterry, L. E. T. Jones, B. Edwards, D. A. G. Ackerman, P. J. Davies, R. T. Evans.

Referee: Ivor David (Neath).

Ireland v Wales, 1952

Lansdowne Road, Dublin, March 8, 1952

When Wales won the championship and Triple Crown in 1969, the emotions of followers and officials were aroused and many were tempted to ajudge the side as the best Welsh XV since the War. It was a good one, certainly, and one would not wish to detract from its performance but, after close analysis of previous sides, I feel both the 1935-36 and the 1951-52 sides were slightly superior. One does not suggest this lightly, or as any criticism of the 1969 side which was superior to all except France, but the two previous sides achieved notable performances and had they enjoyed the advantages of squad coaching their potential, which was considerable, would have been truly fulfilled.

The 1935-36 side defeated New Zealand at Cardiff in quite the most memorable international match since 1905; it drew with England at Swansea, and then defeated Scotland and Ireland for the championship. The match against Ireland was a tremendous affair, decided by a penalty goal kicked by Vivian Jenkins, the only score of the match. The 1951-52 side was a shade more powerful than the unbeaten one of 1949-50, and it possessed an experienced, dominating pack. Indeed, I would suggest that it was the best pack of many good ones produced since the War.

The side lost, narrowly, the match to decide the 'Championship of the World' against South Africa at Cardiff in the

December, and then went on to beat the other four countries in the European championship. At Dublin against Ireland it turned on a remarkable display of power and speed, with forwards and backs working well together and, under the leadership of John Gwilliam, displayed touches of the mobile power rugby that is now dominating the game. Not as ruthless, perhaps, as present-day New Zealanders but expert, swift and confident, playing as if they really enjoyed it.

Both Ireland and Wales were in line for the Triple Crown and Ireland were a strong side at the time, led by D. J. O'Brien at No. 8 with T. Clifford, K. Mullen, J. H. Smith, P. J. Lawlor and J. S. McCarthy to support him at forward, and Kyle and O'Meara at half-back to direct tactical operations. At the time Kyle was the best outside-half in the game and, with his brother-in-law, N. J. Henderson, at centre, as strong and determined as ever. In the side were five 1950 Lions who were well-acquainted with the Welsh approach, and Wales included seven 1950 Lions and four others who were to be honoured in 1955. W. R. Willis, who suffered a broken jaw in the Scottish match, had to stand down and break his sequence of appearances at scrum-half but his deputy, W. A. Williams, was a durable, experienced player with a good service. A. Thomas and M. C. Thomas were paired in the centre as a young partnership, while K. J. and Lewis Jones were two match-winning wings. C. I. Morgan at outside-half was steadily developing as the natural successor to Kyle for world rating.

Yet before the match, played in perfect conditions at Lansdowne Road, where the turf is always immaculately green, everything depended upon the outcome of the forward struggle. The Irish pack under O'Brien was mobile and fiery and capable of disturbing the rhythm of any side. The Welsh pack under Gwilliam was expert at the line-out and good in the tight-loose play. It was big and heavy with a solid front row composed of D. M. Davies as hooker, who shared the Tests with Mullen as a Lion in 1952, and two converted second-row men in D. J. Hayward and W. O. Williams. As an eight it had put up a formidable display against the Springboks and the recall of R. C. C. Thomas gave it added mobility and expertise in the loose.

The Welsh forwards were determined to deny possession to Ireland and dominate in their own way, by committing the lighter Irish flank forwards to work in the tight and thus clear the mid-field for the Welsh backs to operate more freely. Thousands of Welsh followers were in support, resembling a 'Scarlet invasion', for it was the first match played by Wales after a break of 25 years in the City of Dublin where the hospitality is warm and cheering.

Wales achieved a notable victory, resulting from the fine display of the forwards, by a goal, a penalty and two tries to a penalty, and it was in the first half that they achieved control, even though one felt they eased back towards the end of the match instead of celebrating with a feast of scoring. Much of this was due to injuries to players which were not appreciated until after the match, for Stephens developed back trouble; Hayward injured neck and shoulder muscles; Forward burst a blood vessel in his ankle and Morgan pulled a calf muscle. Yet during the first half the side reached the heights of true power and efficiency.

It was the teamwork of the Welsh side that proved so vital, and the many outstanding players in the team—seven of them were to gain more than 20 caps apiece before they retired—blended well into the team effort. This was due to Gwilliam as captain, who maintained the discipline within his ranks which is so necessary for success in rugby, but especially for Welsh sides. I recall congratulating him in the dressing-rooms afterwards but he merely answered, 'It is the other 14 you want to praise, for I am merely the general in charge. They are the troops and match-winners!' This was typically Gwilliam, who will remain one of the outstanding leaders at international level, even though different in approach from many other successful captains.

The Welsh forwards swarmed in the loose like giant bees scattering all before them. John was supreme as an all-round forward, reaching a new peak in his notable career; Stephens got a fine try; Williams and Hayward delved constantly in the tight for possession and Thomas made a successful come-back to international rugby after three years absence while D. M. Davies, once again, was as good as his Lions captain, Karl Mullen. Yet the Irish for all their lack of weight, stuck to it manfully, and were never outshoved in the set scrums. It was strange that such a big strong pack as was fielded by Wales never mastered the art of scrummaging in the fullest sense, although in December it had held its own with the Springbok pack, one of the best to visit the shores of Britain.

Desmond O'Brien led his pack valiantly and never spared himself in trying to curtail the activities of the Welsh, but at the line-out and in the loose the Irish could not dominate as they had done in 1948-49 and 1951. Karl Mullen had lost some of his fire in his 25th appearance for Ireland; rather sadly, it was his last, but he was not to be lost to the game and served it well later as an administrator and selector.

In the battle at half-back, the Welsh pair had the advantage because they received a better service and were under less pressure, but in this match Morgan did take over the mantle from Kyle. The baton was passed from a great player, already established and never to be forgotten, to another younger player on the threshold of greatness. Morgan made one spectacular try by sending Jones on a long run for the Irish line, but Kyle was to play another four times for Ireland against Wales and was only once on the winning side. Six times did Kyle and Morgan oppose each other at inter-national level and Morgan was on the winning side four times, Kyle once, with one match drawn. Yet I do not want to say one was better than the other, but prefer to say that Kyle was on top from 1947 to 1951 and then Morgan from 1952 to 1958—the year they both retired from the scene.

In this match Morgan showed the defence of Cleaver and the attack of Cliff Jones, two of his illustrious Rhondda predecessors, while Ken Jones and Lewis Jones on the wings proved themselves match-winners. Malcolm and Alun

Thomas in the centre tackled like demons and Gerwyn Williams revealed his style and accuracy at full-back. Henderson tried his hardest to crash through the Welsh centres but he could not do so and Ireland had to give best. It is strange that since 1951 Ireland have never been able to top the Championship Table, despite the fact that many famous players have worn the green jersey with its shamrock emblem. They have come near on many occasions and never nearer than in 1969, only to find Wales denying them the final glory, as indeed they have denied it to Wales on several occasions!

Wales took the lead after only eight minutes of play. Wing forward Dargan fell offside in the loose and Lewis Jones with the casualness always associated with his kicking, landed a superb goal from near the touch-line. Next there was a strong dash from the end of the line-out by R. C. C. Thomas, and Stephens remained with him to take the pass and cover the last 15 yards for a try that was not converted by Jones.

Then came the best try of the match. Ireland were attacking in the Welsh '25' but Wales heeled from a scrum and a long pass sent Morgan away at speed. He swerved outwards before straightening-up and then, having got through the Irish defence near the scrum, he raced on to draw Murphy at full-back, committing him to a tackle before handing on to Ken Jones, racing up at his elbow. Jones had a long way to go with Phipps and Chambers chasing him, but gradually, like the Olympic runner he was, Jones pulled away and scored a fine try way out on the left. Even pressmen stood to cheer this fine effort!

Wales led by nine points at the interval and this lead was reduced by three points when the Irish fullback, J. G. Murphy, landed a good penalty goal after Wales had failed to play the ball in a tackle. However, Wales produced another fine forward effort which earned them a try, for Roy John gathered a ball that went loose after a scrummage and raced away like a threequarter.

So successful was John with his swerving and dodging that he deceived several would-be tacklers and reached Murphy at full-back before handing on to R. C. C. Thomas who took the inside pass and scored. Lewis Jones kicked the goal, easily, and the task was too great for Ireland to get back on terms, hard though they tried to disturb a confident Welsh side.

The Teams

Ireland: J. G. M. Murphy (Dublin Univ); W. H. Millar (Queen's Univ.), N. J. Henderson (Queen's Univ.), R. R. Chambers (Instonians), G. C. Phipps (Rosslyn Park); J. W. Kyle (Queen's Univ.), J. O'Meara (Univ. Coll., Cork); T. Clifford (Young Munster), K. Mullen (Old Belvedere), J. H. Smith (Collegians), A. O'Leary (Cork Constitution), P. J. Lawlor (Clontarf), J. S. McCarthy (Dolphin), D. J. O'Brien (Cardiff) capt., M. Dargan (Old Belvedere).

Wales: G. Williams (Llanelli); B. L. Jones (Llanelli), A. Thomas (Cardiff), M. C. Thomas (Newport), K. J. Jones (Newport); C. Morgan (Cardiff), W. A. Williams (Newport); D. J. Hayward (Newbridge), D. M. Davies (Somerset Police), W. O. Williams (Swansea), R. John (Neath), J. R. G. Stephens (Neath), A. Forward (Pontypool), J. A. Gwilliam (Edinburgh Wanderers) capt., R. C. C. Thomas (Swansea).

Referee: P. F. Cooper (England).

Wales v New Zealand, 1953

Cardiff Arms Park, December 19, 1953

History used to repeat itself in Welsh rugby, especially as far as New Zealand was concerned at the Cardiff Arms Park. It is true that Wilson Whineray's team of 1963 and Brian Lochore's team of 1967 changed the course of history, but with far less excitement than in the 'good old days'. Their victories, to lay the Arms Park bogy, were so academic as to

be cold and lustre-lacking, and the large crowds that witnessed them had little to remember when the matches had
ended. Both victories were deserved by New Zealand, and
Welshmen have no complaint in this respect, except, perhaps,
to mourn the absence of traditional Celtic greatness!

It was not so in 1905, 1935 and 1953, when Wales gained
narrow, but exciting, victories, and both sides played with
skill, verve and flourish. They are three matches to remember, not only because Wales beat their great rivals, but
because there was drama in each, with pulsating scores that
made the blood tingle. Great moments, great players and
much creative skill displayed to elevate many players of both
countries to the status of heroes. Teddy Morgan and Bob
Deans of 1905 became household words; Wilfred Wooller
and George Gilbert of 1935, and Ken Jones and Bob Scott of
1953 were indicative of the spirit of individual endeavour
in which players raised the game to a particularly high
standard and captured the imagination with their approach.
It was truly rugby in red and black!

The score was 3-0 to Wales in 1905, and what a match that
was, while 1935 produced an even more exciting one, with
the score 13-12 to Wales. This remains the most thrilling
game of rugby I have been privileged to watch, north of the
equator, and as good as the magnificent 23-22 First Test win
of the British Lions in 1955 at Ellis Park. Such matches have
given to rugby union football a particular status almost un-
equalled in any other amateur team game. To have lived
through both is something of an achievement!

Thus, when the 1953-54 All Blacks under R. C. 'Bob'
Stuart arrived in Europe they had a special image to
maintain, and defeats at Cardiff to avenge, and were determined to succeed where others had failed. It was for them a
formidable challenge and they were mindful of it, from the
very moment their plane touched down at London Airport.
Only one New Zealand side, that of 1924-25, had escaped
from Wales without defeat. Would the fourth All Blacks
succeed?

Above: Wales v New Zealand 1953. W. O. Williams, the Welsh prop, steals away from a maul pursued by R. C. Stuart, the All Blacks captain. *Below:* South Africa and British Lions at Pretoria, 1955. Gareth Griffiths, the Lions right wing, tackled a foot short of the goal line. Jeff Butterfield (right) watches carefully!

New Zealand v British Isles, Dunedin 1959. A stern maul, with
Referee Fleury awarding one of the many penalties in the match.

France v South Africa, 1961. The French forwards peel off to the
blindside of a line-out at Stade Colombes.

The Welsh were coming to the end of a rather successful era, although five of her leading players were to prove themselves outstanding Lions in 1955. Several great players were, however, nearing the end of their colourful careers. These included Gerwyn Williams, Ken Jones, Bleddyn Williams, Rex Willis, D. M. Davies, J. A. Gwilliam and Roy John, but they were still going well in December 1953!

The Cardiff club had done a good job of work in maintaining the Arms Park bogy by defeating the Fourth All Blacks in the first of three visits to the ground, in the seventh match of the tour by 8 points to 3, scoring a goal and a try to a penalty goal. This was a remarkable match, full of fine play in the first half and tremendous tension in the second and Cardiff's effort was recognised with five backs and one forward in the National XV. Bleddyn Williams was the captain, as he had been of Cardiff, and there was only one new cap in Dr. Gwyn Rowlands, who was to play an important part in the match with his accurate place-kicking.

The All Blacks' captain, R. C. Stuart, only declared himself fit two days before the match following blood-poisoning, and the back division was a safety first one, not including the lively Wellington mid-field runners. Obviously, the New Zealand selectors placed their faith in the powerful pack of forwards led by Stuart, and indeed they did enough to earn victory. What then, went wrong?

It was the back division that failed to win the match against a determined defence and the All Blacks reckoned without a remarkable Welsh recovery after it appeared almost inevitable that they would lose. As in 1935, the All Blacks were leading well into the second half, only to be pipped at the post by a thrilling Welsh try which will go down in history. The man who scored it was Ken Jones, on the right wing, who was playing in his 31st match and who had done so well in New Zealand with the 1950 Lions. He was aided and abetted by wing forward R. C. C. Thomas, who had helped Swansea frighten the All Blacks seven days previously in a 6-all draw.

Wales snatched a thrilling win from the All Blacks as they were putting the cup of victory to their lips, and as New Zealand said afterwards, it was the eight fiery Welsh dragons who, eventually turned the game. It was a desperate and thrilling international match; desperate because for three-quarters of the play Wales looked like losing, and thrilling because the Welshmen staged a tremendous revival to achieve victory.

In the first hour of the match, Welsh followers were despondent, for the All Blacks were on top. Wales went into the lead with a try by Judd, converted by Rowlands, as the pair had done for Cardiff in November. Then Jarden, a sadly neglected wing in attack, landed a magnificent penalty goal from near the touchline, before Clarke got a try for New Zealand after a high kick ahead by Scott. Jarden kicked the goal and the half-time score was 8-5 in his side's favour. This time it appeared as if the course of the Cardiff-New Zealand match would be repeated, only in favour of the All Blacks.

Early in the second half Wales lost centre Griffiths with a dislocated shoulder for ten minutes, but it was replaced and the player returned. The pack were eight in number again, but still the All Blacks hammered away and only a tackle of Fitzpatrick by three defenders, Willis and the two Williamses, held him up to prevent a try.

The Welsh survived—just—and lifted the siege of their goal-line to move into the All Blacks' half of the field. Two fine touch-finders by Bleddyn Williams helped their progress and, at a scrum, the All Blacks were penalised for handling the ball, although the player concerned appeared to collapse, unintentionally, as the scrum wheeled. Rowlands kicked the goal and the scores were level at 8-8.

This was the signal for the Welsh revival, the floodgates of Celtic enthusiasm were opened and the scarlet jerseys poured through to harass the surprised All Blacks. From being the attackers they became the defenders and desperate ones at that—for the situation had changed completely.

The Welsh forwards suddenly roused themselves to a special effort and they drove through, down the left touchline, where Elsom was tackled in possession inside his own '25'. R. C. C. Thomas gathered the ball as it went loose and considered several manoeuvres before turning round and punting across field. However, he had drawn Scott out to the wing with Elsom and the switching of the attack caught the All Blacks unawares.

Ken Jones raced in at speed to gather a favourable bounce and swerve inside Jarden to race over the line to the right of the posts for the winning try that was to become an historic one. As in 1905 and 1935, the crowd erupted and had barely subsided by the time Rowlands had converted. The final whistle soon sounded and the crowd invaded the field while players wrestled for the ball which was collected, eventually, by Scott. Wales had won another memorable match against New Zealand, but it was to be the last for many years. On the next two occasions the New Zealand forwards made certain of victory!

The Teams

Wales: G. Williams (London Welsh); K. J. Jones (Newport), G. Griffiths (Cardiff), B. L. Williams (Cardiff) capt., G. Rowlands (Cardiff); C. I. Morgan (Cardiff), W. R. Willis (Cardiff); C. C. Meredith (Neath), D. M. Davies (Somerset Police), W. O. Williams (Swansea), E. R. John (Neath), J. A. Gwilliam (Gloucester), S. Judd (Cardiff), J. R. G. Stephens (Neath), R. C. C. Thomas (Swansea).

New Zealand: R. W. H. Scott; R. A. Jarden, J. Tanner, A. E. G. Elsom; B. B. J. FitzPatrick, L. S. Haig; K. Davis; K. L. Skinner, R. C. Hemi, I. J. Clarke, G. N. Dalzell, R. A. White, R. C. Stuart (capt.), W. A. McCaw, W. H. Clark.

Referee: Dr. P. F. Cooper (R.F.U.).

South Africa v British Isles, 1955

Loftus Versfeld, Pretoria, September 3, 1955

Pretoria, the sun-drenched administrative centre of South Africa, has a rugby atmosphere much akin to that of Llanelli, and the Loftus Versfeld ground there has been the scene of many remarkable matches and incidents concerning touring teams. Its surface is dry, hard, and generally brown in colour during the winter months because of the heavy night frosts. By day the sun shines strongly, and spectators can sit in their shirt-sleeves in the high stands, unashamedly partisan, willing their side to victory.

The 1955 Lions, possibly the best British side to visit South Africa, shared in two exciting matches at Pretoria, and will remember the ground with considerable pleasure. They achieved a last-minute victory over the Northern Transvaal on the Saturday before the Third Test of the tour, which prepared them for the test that has come to be known as the 'Moonlight Sonata' match. Each side had achieved a victory in the two Tests already played and thus this one was to be an important decider and a pointer as to which way the series would go. The Lions had achieved a 23-22 victory in the First Test at Ellis Park, Johannesburg, in what is now regarded as the 'greatest test of all time', while the Springboks achieved a splendid victory through running rugby in the Second Test at Cape Town.

Thus the Third Test at Pretoria promised a battle of tactics, and the absence through injury of both the touring party's captain and vice-captain, Robin Thompson and Angus Cameron, was to play an important part in the events that followed. Their absence gave the mercurial Cliff Morgan the chance to establish himself as one of the top players of his era in world rugby, by leading the British Lions to a famous victory. For him it was his 'greatest hour' in the game.

84

The week of the match proved to be an exciting one, for the South African coach, Danie Craven, was as determined that the Springboks should take the lead in the series as was Jack Siggins and his players to prevent them doing so. Since the first two Tests had produced remarkable running rugby, one sensed that both sides would place a greater emphasis upon defence and engage in more tactical kicking. The Springboks prepared to contain the brilliant Lions' midfield attackers, while the Lions intended to use the touch-line more frequently to keep the Springbok forwards heavily engaged and, if possible to get them moving backwards and thus reduce their effectiveness in the loose.

The Springboks engaged in what is now an historical pre-match training session, in the dark at the Loftus Versfeld ground on the Thursday evening before the match, and the well-known South African sporting columnist, Paul Irwin, christened it the 'Moonlight Sonata', while an Afrikaans paper carried the headline, 'Dr. Craven foils the spies'. The spy in this case was myself and I was much amused, and indeed honoured, at the treatment afforded me by one of my closest friends in the game, Dr. Craven!

Unfortunately for South Africa, their magnificent No. 8 forward Daan Retief had to withdraw through injury and his place was taken by Butch Lochner. This was a loss to them because Retief, as he was to prove in New Zealand in 1956, was a superb ball player in his position. The Lions fielded a side which had Morgan as captain and W. O. Williams of Swansea as pack leader. The illustrious tourist Tom Reid, played in the second-row in place of Thompson and Clem Thomas appeared in his first Test on the flank. As the team had a strong Welsh flavour, with eight players in action, it was wise that the captaincy and pack leadership should have gone to Morgan and Williams, who planned their tactics carefully.

It was a perfect day for rugby and most of the South African Cabinet were sitting in the front row of the stand with their Prime Minister, 'The Lion of the North', Mr.

J. G. Strydom. The atmosphere, although tense, was a happy one. All tickets had been sold well in advance and the 45,000 crowd cheered lustily as the two teams took the field— the Lions headed by Cliff Morgan and the Springboks by another fine player, Stephen Fry. The referee was Ralph Burmister who had proved the best of many sound officials during the tour.

The Lions had won the toss in the dressing-room beforehand and the early period of the game was comparatively tame, following the lively starts of the first two Tests, even though that magnificent forward Johaan Claassen went near with a long-range penalty for the Springboks. Then Morgan probed several times for the gap but found the way barred by an alert covering defence. All were surprised that Griffiths was playing on the right wing and O'Reilly on the left, which was contrary to selection, but this had been done by Morgan at the last moment to keep O'Reilly away from the Springbok right wing, Von Vollenhoven, who had scored three tries against O'Reilly, not necessarily because of O'Reilly, in the Second Test, and this decision proved to be a wise one on the part of Morgan.

Gareth Griffiths, who had flown out as a substitute following the injury to Arthur Smith, almost got over for the Lions after 10 minutes' play when he was tackled just short of the goal-line after beating full-back Dryburgh. Douglas Baker, an excellent outside-half playing at full-back for the Lions because of injury to Cameron and Alun Thomas, went near with a drop at goal, and Claassen was wide again with another long-range penalty attempt. Then, when it seemed that noone was going to score, the Lions executed a perfect back movement to produce a try by O'Reilly, only for the Lions' touch-judge Johnnie Williams to indicate that O'Reilly had just stepped into touch!

Just before half-time the Lions did take the lead in a most unusual manner. The ball came back from a line-out and during a Lions' passing movement a pass went astray, only to be snapped up quickly by Butterfield who, to the surprise of everyone on the ground including his team-mates, checked himself and dropped a neat left-footed goal. It proved to be his first in any form of football with his left foot, but it was an invaluable kick and supplied an urgent need for his side at just the right moment.

The Springboks made tremendous efforts in the second half to draw level and there was much hard, but clean, play. The Lions went further ahead after 10 minutes when Baker landed a good 30-yard penalty, only for the Springboks to reduce the arrears with a fine dropped penalty by Dryburgh, who lazily swung his leg from five yards inside his own half. The Lions were soon back on the attack and from a loose scrum Robins gathered the ball and darted diagonally left to the wide blind side. When challenged, he handed on to the supporting Butterfield outside him, who raced to the corner to get the touch down before he was swept into the corner flag. A smart and sharply taken try.

Baker could not convert it and midway through the second half Dryburgh kicked his second penalty with a place kick from 45 yards, and the Springboks were back in the game. Another penalty award gave Dryburgh a chance to level the scores, but this time his drop-kick sailed wide. An attempt at dropped goal by outside-half Rosenberg was cleverly blocked by Thomas, moving quickly off the side of the scrum. After this the Lions held on to their lead with confidence, despite many strong Springbok attacks. The side remained a cohesive unit in defence, as it had done in attack, with Davies, Griffiths and Baker doing extremely well, and Morgan controlling affairs so efficiently as to earn the title of 'The General'.

At forward, Reid, Courtenay Meredith and the two Williamses were powerful in the set pieces and tight play, while Bryn Meredith, Robins, Greenwood and Thomas were tireless in the loose. While the backs collected the points for the Lions, it was the forwards who laid the foundation of victory—and it takes a good side to beat South Africa twice in any series!

The Teams

South Africa: R. Dryburgh; K. T. Von Vollenhoven, D. J. Sinclair, W. Rosenberg, T. Briers; C. Ulyate, C. Strydom; A. C. Koch, A. Van der Merwe, J. J. Bekker, S. P. Fry (Capt.), J. du Rand, J. Claassen, D. Ackerman, G. P. Lochner.

British Isles: D. G. S. Baker; G. M. Griffiths, J. Butterfield, W. P. C. Davies, A. J. O'Reilly; C. I. Morgan (capt.), R. E. G. Jeeps; W. O. Williams, B. V. Meredith, C. C. Meredith, J. T. Greenwood, R. H. Williams, T. E. Reid, R. C. C. Thomas, R. J. Robins.

Referee: Mr. R. Burmister.

New Zealand v British Isles, 1959

Carisbrook Park, Dunedin, July 18, 1959

Of all the matches I have watched in the last 21 years, the one that keeps coming back like a nightmare is the first Test of the 1959 series between the All Blacks and the Lions. Indeed, one has to be a strong man to relive it without breaking out into a sweat; I cannot recall any single match, played at this level, influenced more by refereeing decisions and the penalty goal. One does not suggest for the moment that there was any intentional effort to prevent the Lions from winning, but I am convinced the whistle obligato of poor Mr. Fleury, the referee, and the accurate big boot of Don Clarke, would have beaten any side in history on this desperate day at Dunedin.

I am wondering how many sides would have remained as calm as did those 1959 Lions, after scoring four fine tries without the opposition crossing their line and losing the match by 18 points to 17. It may have taken a little diplomatic persuasion on the part of his close friends to prevent manager Alf Wilson from bursting forth with a tirade of abuse at the after-match dinner, but I cannot think that any New Zealand management would have taken the result so diplo-

matically, judging by their television reaction when Colin
Meads was sent from the field in Scotland in 1967. All things
are comparative, but having sat with managers Wilson and
Glasgow at Dunedin on this day, I could write almost a
chapter about their amazement at the refereeing decisions,
including suitable expletives! Seven years later, Lions'
manager D. J. O'Brien summed it up rather cleverly when
he said, 'In Test matches in New Zealand, referees appear
to watch the red jerseys in action and not the black.' This
may be true. It cannot be proved, although on this day in
1959 there was really only one side in the game, and they
wore red jerseys.

New Zealanders may not agree with, or enjoy, what I write
about their approach to the game, but in two long tours I
have studied it closely and as a result will continue to press
with all possible fervour for neutral referees. Indeed, con
sidering the manner in which the four home unions lean over
backwards to provide neutrality for touring teams in the
British Isles and France, it seems incredible that New Zealand and South Africa can, on the face of it, continually block
the suggestion of neutral referees at international level. If
it were done, it would ease the burden for everyone and I
am sure British followers would be delighted to welcome
Southern Hemisphere referees to Europe.

The Lions of 1959, as I have recorded elsewhere in this
book, were a much better side even than their record
indicates, and no side deserved more to share a Test series.
Prior to this first Test at Dunedin it had played 13 matches
in Australia and New Zealand, and lost only to New South
Wales and Otago. It played good attractive football and its
forwards did extremely well, providing the backs with plenty
of opportunity to run with the ball. It entered this Test full
of optimism and one felt that should it hold its own at
forward, it would prove much better than the opposition
behind the scrum.

The ground was packed to capacity with a record crowd of
41,500 plus a 'Scotsman's' stand on the adjacent railway bank.

It was the ground where the Lions of 1930 had achieved a memorable 6-3 victory, and the 1950 side a 9-9 draw. Consequently, there were high hopes that these latest Lions would take a lead in the Test series and, of course, they should have done so. The All Blacks, however, went ahead when hooker Dawson was penalised for striking on the full and Clarke landed a straight 40-yard penalty, his first of six.

Four minutes later Scotland, a venturesome, ubiquitous full-back, knocked-on and No. 8 forward Faull played the ball in front of him to have another penalty awarded by Mr. Fleury, and it was an easy kick for big Don Clarke. Half an hour passed before the Lions scored and really looked the attacking force we knew they could be. The All Blacks obstructed at a maul and Hewitt landed a 35-yard penalty, after which a section of the crowd chanted, 'Red, Red, Red!', which was a remarkable tribute to the tourists. These Lions were immensely popular!

Five minutes before the interval they won a scrum on the right-hand side of the field for the shrewd elusive Risman to execute cleverly an opening and send Malcolm Price away. He put the dashing O'Reilly over for a try in the corner that was not converted by Scotland. Before the interval the Lions took the lead when Risman punted to the right corner for the fantastic Peter Jackson to boot ahead over the line and see Price race up and win the touch-down. In the end, poor David Hewitt's failure to convert became a winning margin.

Early in the second half, the big burly second row forward Roddy Evans intercepted a New Zealand pass to pound away and have the support of Ken Smith, who gave Jackson a gallop to the corner and another splendid try. This was winning rugby and the score was now 12-6 in the Lions' favour, but Clarke was still bombarding the Lions' uprights with penalty attempts, and with his third of the second half for an unknown infringement against Jeeps, from bang in front of the Lions' posts, Clarke kicked an easy goal. Even this did not dishearten the roaring Lions and they got another try. All Blacks wing McMullen dropped a pass which Risman gathered smartly to grub-kick ahead and follow the ball on. Ken Scotland was up with him to trap the ball, gather it, and send Price over for his second try which Risman converted easily.

Leading by 17 points to nine with only 10 minutes left for play and with New Zealand never looking like being able to score a try, the odds should have been strongly in favour of the Lions. Even in the stand, however, we knew that Clarke could kick another three goals to carry the day. He was a magnificent kicker and the penalty awards were none of his doing; certainly one could not blame him for grasping at every opportunity to pull his side out of the mire of defeat. Murphy was penalised at a line-out for Clarke to kick his fourth goal and, with seven minutes left for play, another strange penalty award enabled him to kick his fifth. Was this to be the last? No, for with only two minutes left for play, Wood was penalised 30 yards out for allegedly playing the ball in an off-side position. Yet he will swear, even now, that it was first touched by an All Black, while the team captain Ronnie Dawson told me he would have played it himself, had not Wood done so!

Over went the kick and New Zealand were leading 18-17. As if this punishment was not enough even worse was to follow. The Lions rushed the ball to the New Zealand line in a desperate effort to snatch the match out of the fire and Roddy Evans crossed for what appeared to be a perfectly good try—only for the referee to state, 'Handled in the maul!' This decision 'finished us all' and was, as assistant-manager Ossie Glasgow said, 'Incomprehensible!'

Since that day many thousands of words have been written about this match, and in all my travels it is one of only two Test matches that I have seen the Lions lose but really deserve to win. The other was the 'push-over try' match against South Africa at Durban in 1962. How much happier it would have been on each occasion had there been neutral referees in charge. It is so easy to avoid these unhappy controversies and if only New Zealand and South Africa would do what the British do all would be well. The cost of such a departure would be almost negligible. At least give it a go!

The Teams

New Zealand: D. B. Clarke; P. T. Walsh, R. F. McMullen; T. R. Lineen, B. E. Macphail; R. H. Brown, R. J. Urbahn; W. H. Whineray (capt.), R. C. Hemi, I. J. Clarke, I. Mac-Ewan, S. F. Hill, E. A. R. Pickering, P. F. Jones, B. E. L. Finlay.

British Isles: K. J. F. Scotland; P. B. Jacksons, M. Price, D. Hewitt, A. J. F. O'Reilly; A. B. W. Risman, R. E. G. Jeeps; B. G. M. Wood, A. R. Dawson (capt.), H. F. McLeod, W. R. Evans, R. H. Williams, G. K. Smith, J. Faull, N. A. A. Murphy.

Referee: Mr. A. L. Fleury (Otago).

France v South Africa, 1961

Stade Colombes, Paris, February 18, 1961

Rugby matches are often remembered for over-vigorous play and the good football in them is soon forgotten. This has happened on many occasions and in 1969 the Wales-Ireland match at Cardiff was highlighted by three or four incidents while the match itself produced some magnificent rugby, particularly in the second half. However, it is especially true of the memorable match between France and South Africa in 1961, towards the end of a long tour by South Africa in Europe. The Springboks were playing their fifth and final international match and having beaten the four Home Countries were determined to defeat the French, who, at the time, were the reigning champions of Europe, having won the title in 1959.

There was a considerable amount of advance publicity for this match. The French were equally determined to remain unbeaten and, as the Press representatives of both countries contributed to the pre-match build-up, it assumed the importance of a World championship match. Prior to moving on to France, the Springboks had played 30 matches in the British Isles with only one defeat and that in the 30th match against the Barbarians at the Arms Park, when they lost by two tries to nil. The Springboks had been nervous about meeting the Barbarians and had even suggested a match between two sides of players in which Springboks were included in both teams. The defeat was not accepted easily because it was suggested that the Barbarians had played match-winning rugby, but the fact that the Springbok un-beaten record was at stake produced a game of intense excitement and the Barbarians well deserved their victory.

The French had won their two match series in South Africa in 1958 and they were determined to maintain their record, even though the Springboks had beaten South West France 29-3, the French 'B' side 26-10 and a Pyrenees-Basque XV 36-9. In the French side were some outstanding players, all experienced men, while the pack were particularly strong with Domenech, Roques, Crauste, Celaya and Moncla in world class. The South Africans though at the end of their long tour were at full strength and the referee was Mr. Gwynne Walters, who had handled only one previous match during the tour—and that being the controversial one at Cardiff, when the Springboks were criticised for over-vigorous play.

Conditions were perfect when the teams took the field before a larger crowd than usual at Stades Colombes, estimated at nearly 60,000. It is said that the 'black market' in tickets sent the normal prices rocketing to at least six times above their normal value. The Press Box was full of international critics from many countries and even they were surprised at what happened from the first whistle. At the first scrum, a Springbok was kicked and then followed a series of clashes between the four props, Domenech and Roques of France, and du Toit and Kuhn of South Africa. It was a struggle for physical dominance, and for almost 10 minutes, the 'battle' was fought with great fury at forward while the two back divisions watched the proceedings with alarm. It was a fight! Then, suddenly, the diminutive Referee Walters blew a long blast on his whistle and led the two captains away into an open space and spoke to them. He said to Moncla and Malan, 'Either you stop this fighting, or I will abandon the game.' Malan answered politely, 'We want to play rugby!' While the three were in earnest conversation, the large crowd hooted, whistled and booed. Then the two captains returned after receiving the ultimatum, to talk to their respective packs of forwards and the match, which was so near to ending prematurely, continued, to the relief of all concerned.

The final drastic warning by Referee Walters in his greatest hour as an official had the desired effect, and from that moment onwards the match was an exciting struggle between two powerful teams. So well were they matched that neither side could score and the game ended, deservedly, in a draw. Thus France did not lose the title won in South Africa and the Springboks emerged from their five international matches without a defeat. However, there were near misses on the part of both sides as they tried desperately to gain an advantage.

The French pack rose to the occasion magnificently and eliminated all doubt in the minds of their supporters that they would not survive against the powerful and all-conquering Springbok pack that had been held only by Ronnie Dawson's Barbarians. The Springboks enjoyed an advantage at the line-out through the fine jumping of Claassen and Avril Malan, while the French won the tight head count as Domenech, de Gregorio and Roques proved even stronger than du Toit, Abe Malan and Kuhn. In the loose, the French held a slight advantage and some of the close passing developed from the peel-off at the line-out was often outstanding.

The Springboks were not quite as accurate in their handling and kicking and Stewart, at outside-half, normally an immaculate player and a good tactical kicker, lost some of his accuracy and his kicks ahead were more than adequately dealt with by the brilliant French full-back, Vannier. Again, Wilson, usually a model of soundness at full-back for South Africa, failed to match Vannier, and the tackling of the whole French back division was first-class, with Boquet marking Gainsford closely and effectively. It was interesting to see how wisely the French had prepared for this match and the back row work of the Springboks was well-covered.

The French played with the wind in the first half and were rather unlucky not to be leading at the interval. In the second half they came near to scoring when they moved away from a loose scrum and with Boniface through and Rancoule unmarked outside him, the wing dropped the vital pass! How sad this was for France, for in the first half they twice came near to scoring tries, and on one occasion Crauste was just beaten for the touch-down by the ball rolling into touch-in-goal. Albaladejo, the shrewd outside-half, just failed with strong attempts at dropped goals. For South Africa, Lockyer went near with two penalty attempts and Hopwood almost got a try.

However, although a draw was a fair result of this match and honour was satisfied on both sides, it was the French who came nearest to victory. Had they taken their chances they would have won almost comfortably, for their devastating pace in the loose was quite outstanding. On the day, even the best of All Blacks sides could have failed. The Springboks a little tired at the end of their tour pursued a more orthodox course through the game and the fact that they were beaten in the set scrums, and in the loose, allowed them no opportunity to dominate, but they shared in a memorable afternoon's rugby!

The Teams

France: M. Vannier (Chalon), H. Rancoule (Toulon), G. Boniface (Mont de Marsan), J. Bouquet (Vienne), J. Dupuy (Tarbes); P. Albaladejo (Dax), P. Lacroix (Agen); A. Domenech (Brives), J. de Gregorio (Grenoble), A. Roques

(Cahors), M. Crauste (Lourdes), J. P. Saux (Pau), G. Bouguyon (Grenoble), F. Moncla (Pau) capt., M. Celaya (Bordeaux).

South Africa: L. G. Wilson; M. G. Antelme, J. L. Gainsford, A. I. Kirkpatrick, J. P. Engelbrecht; D. A. Stewart, R. J. Lockyer, S. P. Kuhn, G. F. Malan, P. S. du Toit, G. H. van Zyl, A. S. Malan (capt.), J. T. Claassen, M. J. M. Pelser, D. J. Hopwood.

Referee: D. G. Walters (Wales).

N. Transvaal v British Lions, 1968

Pretoria, July 3, 1968

It was reported at the start of the 1968 Lions' tour that No.13 was lucky for former Fleet Air Arm pilot, Manager David Brooks. To some extent this was true, and in one instance the good fortune worked like a charm—in the 13th match of the tour against the powerful Northern Transvaal, who eventually became Currie Cup winners and provincial champions of South Africa.

This match followed the stormy affair at Springs in which the Lions had had poor John O'Shea sent off, quite rightly, for punching after he had been provoked, and then reinstated on the Monday so that he could play in this match. Actually, it was good diplomacy on the part of both parties, for the presence of O'Shea helped to restore common-sense to the tour and led the way for a magnificent game to be played. It was a truly remarkable match, in a manner different from most matches on tour, for the attention was held throughout in a hard, fast, pulsating, but clean contest. First one side was right on top, then the other drew level, and the final stages held the viewers breathless with excitement.

The Northern Transvaal has had a reputation for powerful forward play since the War, supported by clever halves,

Above: British Isles v Northern Transvaal. 1968. Mike Coulman the Lions prop scores an important try after a peel-off from a line-out in the second half. *Below:* Wales v England, 1969. Barry John, the Welsh outside half, emerging from a maul to feed Maurice Richards (out of picture) with a scoring pass.

Above: The 1945/46 Kiwis team in Army uniform before the start of their memorable tour. *Below:* Cardiff. 1947-48. The Champion Welsh club of the season. *Standing (l to r):* W. G. Jones, G. Evans, L. Manfield, W. E. Tamplin, R. Roberts, E. Jones, C. Davies. *Sitting (l to r):* A. D. S. Bowes, D. H. Jones, Dr. J. Matthews, H. Tanner (captain), D. E. Davies (Chairman), B. L. Williams, W. B. Cleaver, R. F. Trott. *In front:* M. James and L. Williams.

and in their ranks were six Springboks, with scrum-half Piet Uys as captain. Their supporters breathed the 'fire of confidence' in the Assembly Hotel and the liaison officers were as kind as it was possible to be, as if they were caring for condemned men about to meet their end. Everything pointed to a heavy defeat for the Lions.

But Kiernan and Telfer, leaders of considerable experience, were equally determined to stand and fight, for it was the 'Alamein' of the tour. There could be no retreat and the match had come to be known as the Fifth Test, which meant that it had to be won if the tour was to retain its full interest until the end!

Again, no touring team in South Africa had beaten the Northern Transvaal in eight years, and this was a formidable record, enough to inspire big, bustling, expert forwards like Frik du Preez, Mof Myburgh, Pitzer and Laurens, to make a special effort for their side, clad in their light blue jerseys, and they did!

Sixty thousand spectators roared with approval as the Northerns pounded away to a comfortable 13-5 lead after the Lions had dared to score first. There appeared no hope, for it was a rugby *blitzkreig*, and the Northerns were magnificently efficient, rampaging in unison, with their pack giving a display in the first half-hour that has not been matched in my humble vision, before or afterwards!

Hearts were low in the Lions' camp—extremely low! Could nothing halt this rugby 'enemy' as it crushed the pride of Britain? Like the *blitzkreig* columns, the Northerns stretched themselves just too far and the Lions slowed them down, to get to 8-16 at the interval.

The scoring had gone like this—(2 minutes) Lions moved left from a breakdown and Richards kicked back inside to the line to catch the full-back, who started running in goal, lost the ball and Richard got up quickly to score a try that Kiernan converted; (11) After heavy pressure the Northerns forced a scrum-five and No. 8 forward Fourie de Preez picked up at the back of the scrum and dived fiercely to score through a wall of defenders, but the try was not converted by Pretorious; (19) The ball went loose from a line-out and Fourie du Preez chased after it to gather, get tackled, and see the loose ball picked up by Pitzer, who dived over for a try that Pretorious did convert to make it 8-5 against the Lions; (22) the Northerns won a line-out on the left, and Steyn went away to send the ball inside to blind-side wing, Dirksen, bursting through like an arrow, and he gave to Flemix, who sent Fourie du Preez dashing over for his second, and a superb, try. Pretorious converted and the difference between the sides was inconceivable at 13-5.

How could the Lions survive? The Northerns were almost over again, twice, but the Lions held on for 12 minutes and then Kiernan kicked a 30-yard penalty and it was 13-8. Then two minutes from the interval, outside-half Steyn dropped a lovely high goal from 40 yards. It was a beauty and full-back Pretorious was just wide with a 50-yard penalty just like the artillery softening-up for further mobile armoured attacks in the second half!

The score was 16-8 at the restart, but after only two minutes of play came the try that was to turn the match, and it was a sort of 'secret weapon', alas, not to be used again on tour with similar effect. A line-out in the Northerns '25' saw Coulman peel-off and gather Taylor's tap-down to charge to the Northerns line and score an audacious try. Kiernan, with his immaculate accuracy, kicked the goal and it was only 16-13 to the Northerns! However, they were not relinquishing their grip easily and they hammered away vigorously, but cleanly. Telfer was hurt and assisted from the field, bleeding like a stuck pig, and there was little hope now, even though Delme Thomas left the stand to get ready to take the field.

Ten minutes passed without a substitute before the ice-cool Kiernan, a true captain, levelled the scores with a 40-yard penalty. It was now 16-16 and Telfer returned bandaged like an Egyptian mummy; the struggle was really on with 15 minutes to go. The Lions, at long last, went ahead when Kiernan put over his third penalty goal, this time from 26 yards, and three minutes later he kicked his fourth, a beauty from 40 yards, and it was 22-16!

Not to be outdone, Pretorious landed an even-better one from 50 yards and it was 22-19. He got his chance to level the scores again, in injury time, but from 35 yards he kicked wide and the final whistle was sounded to herald a notable Lions' victory. Easily the best of the tour, it was a credit to both teams and did much to restore the happy passage of the Lions, at least until after the visit to East London!

Kiernan got 16 points to add to the 17 points he collected on the same ground in the First Test. They should have called it Loftus Kiernan, in recognition of his superb kicking, but it was a team effort, with Gibson playing his best match in what was for him an indifferent tour. No wonder there were celebrations that 'raised the roof' of the Assembly Hotel, as the Lions roared!

The Teams
Northern Transvaal: D. Pretorious; K. Meiring, M. Neuhoff, J. Flemix, C. Dirksen; P. Steyn, P. Uys (capt.); J. L. Myburgh, G. Pitzer, R. Potgeiter, O. du Pitsanie, J. J. Spies, F. C. du Preez, T. Laurens, F. du Preez.

British Isles: T. J. Kiernan (capt.); K. F. Savage, T. G. R. Davies, F. K. P. Bresnihan, M. C. R. Richards; C. M. H. Gibson, R. M. Young; J. P. O'Shea, J. V. Pullin, M. J. Coulman, P. K. Stagg, P. F. Larter, R. J. Arneil, J. W. Telfer, R. B. Taylor.

Referee: M. W. Odendaal (Pretoria).

Wales v England, 1969

Cardiff Arms Park, April 12, 1969

The 1969 international season was highlighted through the introduction of a special squad system by Wales, with the leading players limited, voluntarily, to one match a week. It was revolutionary in the Union game in the British Isles, much criticised at first, but it carried Wales to her last match of the season unbeaten, and she faced England at the Cardiff Arms Park in April in line for both the Championship and the Triple Crown.

England had lost to Ireland, narrowly, but defeated both France and Scotland to stand in line for the Championship if Wales could be beaten. Thus it was a match of promise, for the England back row threatened to keep the Welsh halves in check, and the threequarters, spearheaded by Duckham and Webb, promised to score the points for victory, while the big right boot of full-back Hiller was certain to capitalise upon any Welsh errors.

At Porthcawl, during the pre-match work-out, the Englishmen were quietly confident and the chairman of selectors, officiating for the last time before retiring from the role, Mickey Steele-Bodger, told me, 'We have come to win this match. Two years ago Wales robbed us of the Triple Crown, so we'll do it tomorrow!' In 1967 Wales won a remarkable match by 34 points to 21, but little did we think that she would repeat the performance with an even more convincing display of swift running and skilful rugby!

Scotland were beaten more thoroughly than the score of 17-3 suggested; Ireland were routed by 24-11 after a fierce struggle in the first half in the presence of the Prince of Wales, but France, with a new captain in Spanghero and their best display of the season, held Wales to an 8-8 draw. Thus 49 points had been scored with 22 against and only twice had the Welsh line been crossed against nine tries scored by Wales. This was a margin that suggested tough work ahead for the England defence.

However, Wales were without their captain, Brian Price, suffering from a knee injury, and speedy centre Gerald Davies, injured at the end of the French match, with a dislocated elbow, and it was anticipated their absence would upset the balance of a side that had played three matches unchanged without defeat. The assumption proved incorrect, for John Dawes at centre and Delme Thomas in the second row, were players of considerable experience and, more important, members of the national training squad. They knew exactly what was required of them, while Gareth Edwards, who took over the responsibility of captaincy in the absence of Price, had done the job before in the previous season at the age of 20. He was the ideal competitor—confident, expert, strong and elusive—and it was his approach that formulated the pattern of the Welsh victory. Edwards subjugated his natural individual brilliance in the cause of the team, thereby proving himself a far shrewder player tactically than his effervescent individualistic play had suggested previously.

For Maurice Richards it was a remarkable match, since he scored four tries to equal a 70-year-old record by the oldest surviving Welsh international, Willie Llewellyn, who watched the performance on television. The speed, anticipation and elusive running of Richards, especially for his last try, proved too much for the England defence, committed to extra duty as a result of the failure of the first five, or tight, English forwards. They failed in their task, even with the wind in their favour, and as the English halves were not able to read the game tactically, what possession they received was not used wisely. They kicked unimaginatively instead of making the most of their threequarter line.

In the first half, when they were fresh and playing with the wind, the English forwards should have achieved and maintained an advantage, but the better-drilled and stronger Welsh first five neutralised the situation into a stalemate, as intended. At the line-out, the Welshmen, with Delme Thomas as a spearhead, dominated, and at the set scrums they shoved and wheeled to upset the rhythm of the English heel. In the loose they harassed and made it extremely difficult for the back-row of Taylor, Rollitt and Rogers to get into the game as attackers. Brian Thomas, in his first international as pack-leader for Wales, was a host in himself and the effort he and his tireless colleagues made during the first half really won the match for Wales. England were denied the points they needed so desperately and could achieve no more than a penalty goal by Hiller.

Wales scored a try in the first half by Richards following good approach work by Watkins, Denzil Williams, Young and John. Early in the second half, Jarrett kicked a penalty and another shortly afterwards to put Wales well in the lead. Then came a superb try by John, who weaved through four defenders in 30 yards, for Jarrett to convert, and England were right back on the defensive. They could not stop the Welsh machine, and tries came at regular intervals.

Richards got his second try before Hiller kicked his second penalty and then John dropped a goal. Richards got his third try, which Jarrett converted, and then came the fourth, and best, try by Richards, also converted by Jarrett. Hiller got his third penalty and the final score was 30-9. All that Wales intended to do was achieved, and the after match celebrations were much enjoyed. England paid tribute to the Welsh who were to taste, seven weeks later, the full power, strength and ruthlessness of New Zealand rugby. Only then were we able to appreciate the difference in approach, strength and skill existing between the Southern and Northern Hemispheres in the game. It was indeed a moment of truth!

The Teams

Wales: J. P. R. Williams; S. J. Watkins, K. S. Jarrett, S. J. Dawes, M. C. R. Richards; B. John, G. O. Edwards (capt.); D. Williams, J. Young, D. J. Lloyd, W. D. Thomas, B. Thomas, W. D. Morris, T. M. Davies, J. Taylor.

England: R. Hiller; K. C. Plummer, J. S. Spencer, D. J. Duckham, R. E. Webb; J. F. Finlan, T. C. Wintle; D. L. Powell, J. V. Pullin, K. E. Fairbrother, N. E. Horton, P. F. Larter, R. B. Taylor, D. M. Rollitt, D. P. Rogers (capt.).

Referee: D. P. d'Arcy. (I.R.U.)

PART THREE

The Teams

The 1945-46 Kiwis

It would be just to state that one of the most popular teams to visit the British Isles was the 1945-46 Kiwis side under the captaincy of Charles Saxton and the management of Col. A. H. Andrews. It is true that they toured under special circumstances and were like rugby manna from Heaven in a country starved of big football for five years as a result of World War II. However, the Kiwis fulfilled their task successfully by helping to restore peace-time conditions and atmosphere to the rugby game in the four home unions, and for this British rugby men will be ever grateful.

The team brought with it a refreshing breeze of peace-time sport, and its unbounded zest for the game, the cheerfulness of its players and the quality of its play earned it the ready praise of opponents and critics. The members of the party are still a proud group, holding a special place in our rugby memories, and although they may never receive the full praise due to them in their own country, they will be remembered always at Twickenham, Cardiff Arms Park, Lansdowne Road and Murrayfield.

One of the team's staunchest supporters is the effervescing Winston McCarthy, who toured with them as a sound radio commentator and established himself as one of the quickest and most accurate members of his profession during the tour. He has recorded his love for the Kiwis in his cheerful book *Rugby in My Time*. He says, 'Anyhow, to anyone who wants to say that I was a one-eyed Kiwi man, I'm going to say proudly: "Too right I was—and I am".' McCarthy was caught up in the gaiety and happiness of the tour, which has not been emulated to the same extent by succeeding New

Zealand tours. This is regrettable, for the Kiwi spirit was magnificent.

John Daniell, who was then President of the Rugby Football Union, praised them in a particular way when he said, 'British rugby was not prepared to receive the visit of such a highly trained and efficient side.' This is true, but the glamour of the tour and the desire of British opposition to do battle with such famous and friendly rivals encouraged teams to make the best use of their resources. If it was a blood transfusion, it was a painless one, and having spent much time with these tourists, and watched them play many of their matches, especially while on demobilisation leave, I grew to admire them as players and as men. They were the best that New Zealand could produce, in war and peace, and after serving the Allied cause in North Africa and Italy, they returned to the Mother Country to celebrate the peace as only sportsmen can, by producing their best on the field of play.

When they returned home, sixteen of their party of 32 players became full All Blacks and four of them—Saxton, Finlay, Allen and Boggs—became close friends of mine. They are devoted Kiwi-believers and have always desired that rugby football should be a running game. The fact that many of the Kiwis toured with the 1949 All Blacks in South Africa produced a 'tactical split' in the touring camp. Faced by tremendous pressure from a powerful South African pack and the accuracy of place-kicker Okey Geffin, much of the desire of the All Blacks to run was stifled and Allen and his men were able on only a few occasions to produce the attractive Kiwi style. Naturally, there was disappointment at this experience, and the beaten New Zealand team, white-washed in the four-test series, returned home determined to concentrate entirely on forward play. As Allen once told me, 'I saw the gallows on the quay-side when the ship reached Wellington harbour!'

Following this 'national disaster' the Kiwis were out of favour, but, like the good soldiers they were, Saxton and

Allen fought back to inspire New Zealand to get as near as possible to the Kiwi approach when they managed the 1967 medium-length tour in Europe. Allen was ready to retire from active service after this, satisfied that he had proved his point that New Zealand could have fast running backs as well as powerful forwards, and that rugby football was a fifteen-a-side game rather than a ten-man one.

During the five-months Kiwi tour, 27 matches were played with 23 won, two lost and two drawn. A total of 484 points were scored for, and 147 against, and only Scotland and Monmouthshire were successful against them, although Leinster and Newport shared honourable draws. At the start of the tour, only two players, Saxton and Finlay, the captain and vice-captain, had established reputations in New Zealand, but the players under their care were full of enthusiasm and, during the tour, developed the one vital factor that makes great sides, a true sense of team spirit, and this was maintained to the very end of the tour. The experience helped many of the younger players to return home as established ones and New Zealand rugby got away to a fine start after the interval of the War years.

Before each match played, the three tour selectors, Stewart, Butler and Hoare, impressed upon the players that the passing game was the true secret of successful rugby and the two mid-field stars, Allen and Smith, saw to it that these tactics were observed. The basic principle of open play brought its reward in two outstanding tries, one in the second half in the Combined Services match, when Woolley got the touch-down, and the other against Aberavon in the final match of the tour, scored by Kearney. On these occasions, memories of the 1924 Invincibles were revived and there can be no greater praise than this.

The Kiwis played many hard matches while on tour, especially in Wales, against Cardiff, Newport and the national fifteen, while they recall still what was for them, the nightmare sight of the famous Monmouthshire 'poacher', Hedley Rowland, scoring three tries against them at Pontypool Park on the occasion of their only defeat in Wales. The match against Cardiff was a tremendous affair, as both teams took the field on Boxing Day, 1945, unbeaten. One side had to lose—and it was Cardiff, by a try, the only score of the game, achieved by Kearney. In the match against Wales, it was a hard struggle until the long-striding wing Sherratt gathered a loose clearing kick and raced 60 yards for a memorable try.

However, as at Pontypool Park, the Kiwis were well-beaten before a crowd of 40,000 at Murrayfield. It was a notable victory for the Scots and the loss of their unbeaten record was almost a relief for the Kiwis. It is said of the side that, had it possessed two giant locks, it could have ranked with the greatest and most attractive ever produced by New Zealand. It came very near to this ideal, as it was, and players to remember include Scott and Cooke at full-back; Argus, Meates, Sherratt and Boggs on the wing; Smith at centre who was quite the most brilliant member of the team; Kearney, Allen and Proctor at five-eighth, and Finlay, known as the Iron Major, Thornton, Simpson, Arnold, Blake and McPhail at forward, while Saxton, as captain, despite a painful shoulder injury, was an inspiration to his side at scrum-half.

The happy tales of the Kiwis' 'off the field' activities are now legendary, but everyone loved them and no side, however great, can enjoy such popularity again with the ordinary rugby supporter. They were the best mixers off the field and the happiest players on the field, ever to visit the British Isles. This, for me, earns them a high place in world ranking. Their influence on the game was considerable, and they were the only post-War New Zealand side to smile on the field of play. They showed their enjoyment!

Cardiff 1947-48

A well-drilled club side full of brilliant individuals, dedicated to combination, produces the perfect rugby machine and this was true of Cardiff in 1947-48. It was a side blessed with all the qualities of greatness, and wherever it played it attracted record crowds, who were impressed by the confidence, accuracy and personal pleasure the players derived from producing such magnificent rugby.

While Cardiff have never achieved an invincible season they have enjoyed three remarkable ones during which they were lauded as the greatest. Under P. F. Hancock in 1885-86 they played 27, won 26 and lost only one, to Moseley, scoring 533 points with only 14 against. This was the season they employed the four threequarter system to revolutionise back play. Then, in 1905-06, under the leadership of the mercurial P. F. Bush, they played 32 matches and lost only one—to the First N.Z. 'All Blacks', as a result of a 'gift' try—while scoring 513 points against 86. This side had remarkable players, including Gabe and Nicholls at threequarter, and its speed and skill delighted spectators as much as it worried opponents.

The third most successful year for the club came in 1947-48 with Haydn Tanner in charge, and this outstanding player presided over his flock like a senior deacon, providing an outstanding example and image for them to follow, both on and off the field. He was vastly experienced in the game, having achieved all possible honours and was, at the time, the reigning captain of Wales and the world's leading scrum-half. Tanner's knowledge of the game and long experience in many sides, as well as a Lions' tour of South Africa in 1938, fitted him expertly for the task of leadership. In addition, he was a shrewd man and knew well how to get the best out of his team, although never one to suffer fools gladly!

In the 1947-48 season, eleven Cardiff players appeared for

Wales, which remains a record for any club. Only two matches were lost, on September 6 to Pontypool and on March 13 to Penarth, both away from home, and a Cardiff Club record of 803 points were scored with 161 against. The tally of 803 included 182 tries, 84 of which were converted, 23 penalty goals and five dropped goals. Bleddyn Williams, the vice-captain and powerful international side-stepping centre, collected 41 tries to create a new club record, while Les Williams scored 34 and D. H. Jones 22, both strong running wings. The chief place-kicker and pack leader, W. E. Tamplin, amassed 137 points and among the Cardiff victories were 50-5 over Leicester and 41-7 over Plymouth, while Newport were beaten four times in the season. However, the victory most enjoyed was that over the Third Wallabies which maintained the club's record against touring teams.

My admiration for Haydn Tanner had been considerable since his superb performances as a schoolboy for Swansea and Wales against the 1935 New Zealand touring team. To Swansea must go the credit for developing the player, and when he joined Cardiff in 1946 he was right at the top of the rugby tree. Again, the club had played through the War to enjoy an advantage over its rivals in Wales, and Tanner took command of a side already blended with experience and youth and possessing a splendid team spirit.

Of the side he led, Tanner says: 'The real basis for its success was the attacking power of the team as a whole— forwards and backs together. The mid-field triangle of Williams, Matthews and Cleaver would cause any defence a real headache, but one must not forget the support given by such forwards as Cliff Davies—a front row man—Gwyn Evans, Elvet Jones and Les Manfield. The forwards were geared to attack and supplied the ball when it was required, especially when we were in an attacking position. Here, Maldwyn James, as hooker, played his part and in the line-out Bill Tamplin was a tower of strength.

'When the pressure was "on" there was no more intelligent kicker of the ball than Cleaver, while Matthews, in the centre, was capable, through his powerful tackling, of breaking up any attack. Around the scrum we developed a defence which was rarely pierced, and this was due to the highly intelligent play of the back-row, but especially Manfield. Our forwards, possibly, were light for a first-class club pack, but it was a team that was determined to attack on every occasion and defend most capably whenever necessary.'

Besides proving an excellent team, the side sparkled with individuals and of them Tanner says: 'Individuals certainly played a big part in our success, but they were complementary to each other. Williams and Matthews in the centre were so different in approach, but so right for each other. Cleaver was criticised for not being able to pass the ball, but the answer to this strange suggestion is that the team scored over 800 points and he was the pivot player!

'It is true that the individuals were often brilliant, but the backing-up was always superb and I cannot recall one occasion when I broke from the scrum and was not supported by Cleaver or a wing forward—usually by both!

'There was a basic pattern in our play, based on the fact that our attacking back division was better than the opposition. This required that the forwards went on to the field to win the ball for the backs—what is now termed "good ball". If this did not succeed the tactics could be changed easily. It must be appreciated that the game today is the subject of more detailed planning, but in this side our opponents were studied and our tactics discussed before we took the field. All that was needed was to form the plan and the players would adapt their play to the plan. Individuals were instructed to conform to a plan and to work as a member of the team, and I was able to dictate the pattern of play for two reasons: (1) being captain of the side and (2) playing at scrum-half.'

Tanner has always thought deeply about rugby and even today he has lucid comments to make upon affairs, although opportunities to watch have been limited by much intercontinental travel. In comparing the eras before the War and today, he says, 'When I first played for Wales in 1935 the spearhead of the attack was then recognised as the outside-half or first centre. After the War a gradual change took place and the scrum-half and wing-forward came more into the picture in attack, and most of the attacks were created from set pieces. Today the picture has changed still further, and the majority of successful attacks are now developed from second-phase play rather than from the set pieces.

'Thus, in a present-day side, by far the most important factor is the forward strength, while the scrum-half is now more important than ever, since he has more opportunity of running with the ball, and while one regrets it, every side must field an expert place-kicker.'

Cardiff had outstanding players in 1947-48 and they formed a side which bridged the gap between two eras, that before the War and that of today. They did so, brilliantly, and provided tremendous pleasure for many people. Welsh rugby owes this side a debt of gratitude for the influence it had upon the game's revival and development after World War II. Its success remains a remarkable tribute to a remarkable player—Haydn Tanner.

Wales 1950

There is a tradition in Welsh rugby that suggests the national XV is never more dangerous than in the season following the year when it has suffered the ignominy of the Wooden Spoon or a low position in the Championship table. The following year they have often won the Championship. In the season 1948-49, Wales possessed many outstanding players, but failed to click as a team for several reasons. Many senior players reached the end of long and colourful careers and in 1950 new men were introduced into the team to play England at Twickenham in January.

The most revolutionary of selections was the choice of W. R. Willis, of Cardiff as inside-half without having had a

Upper: Wales 1950. The Champion country of the year, achieving the 'grand slam'. *From left, back row:* Mr. I. Jones; Robins; Hayward; John; Evans; Cale; Cleaver. *Front row:* K. Jones; M. Thomas; L. Jones; Gwilliam; Matthews; C. Davies; G. Williams. *On ground from left to right:* R. Willis and D. M. Davies. *Lower:* South Africa 1951-52. The fourth Springboks who lost only one match during their European tour. *(l to r) top row:* G. J. van Wyk, J. Pickard, E. Dinkelmann, J. du Rand, W. Barnard, B. Myburgh, G. Dannhauser, F. van der Ryst, S. Fry. *3rd row:* J. Buchler, J. Bekker, S. Viviers, A. Geffin, P. Wessels, M. Saunders, W. Delport, C. Koch, F. Marais. *2nd row:* A. C. Keevy, J. Brewis, P. A. du Toit, B. Kenyon (capt.), F. Mellish (Mngr.), H. Muller (vice-capt.), D. Craven (Asst. Mngr.), R. Van Schoor, J. K. Ochse. *Front row:* D. Sinclair, J. Oelofse, P. Johnstone, D. Fry, and M. Lategan.

British Isles 1955. *In front:* R. E. G. Jeeps, G. Griffiths, J. E. Williams, T. Lloyd. *Sitting:* W. O. Williams, J. Butterfield, D. E. Davies (Hon. Secretary), R. H. Thompson (captain), J. A. E. Siggins (Manager), A. Cameron (vice-captain), C. I. Morgan, B. V. Meredith. *First row standing:* R. Robins, J. T. Greenwood, A. J. O'Reilly, R. H. Williams, E. J. S. Michie, T. E. Reid, R. C. C. Thomas, R. Roe. *Second row standing:* A. Thomas, H. Morris, C. C. Meredith, F. D. Sykes, A. R. Smith, D. S. Wilson, T. Elliot, D. G. S. Baker. *Back row:* A. C. Pedlow, J. P. Quinn, W. P. C. Davies, H. F. McLeod. (Absent A. R. Higgins.)

trial, and this caused a considerable controversy. Willis had graduated to Cardiff from the Llandaff club and had developed rapidly while serving the clever mid-field triangle of Cleaver, Williams and Matthews. The 'infant prodigy' Lewis Jones, of Devonport Services, who had been introduced to senior rugby by Neath, was a surprise selection at full-back since there was no room for him in an experienced threequarter line of Jones, Matthews, Williams and Thomas, that was later to play as a unit for the British Lions. At forward, there were two new caps in D. M. Davies, of Somerset Police, and J. D. Robins, of Sale and Birkenhead Park. On paper, it looked a good side, but before it took the field two vital changes had to be made as a result of the withdrawal of experienced players Bleddyn Williams and Rees Stephens through illness and injury respectively, and on the morning of the England match these unavoidable changes were expected to weaken the side. However, Welsh selector W. H. Harris confided to me before the kick-off, 'I think we will win and have a wonderful season!'

Into the side went T. J. Brewer, of Oxford University and Newport, on the left wing with Thomas moving into the centre, while Roy John, of Neath, took Stephens's place in the second row. This left Wales with six new caps, and the leadership was given to John Gwilliam, an experienced forward who had already played six times for Wales, and who was to become a big name in the game.

Wales won an exciting match by 11 points to five. Gwilliam's leadership, plus the enthusiasm of the whole side and the initiative of young Lewis Jones, were the main reasons for success. Gwilliam got the Welsh pack moving forward for most of the match, and the backs took full advantage of the situation to record only the first victory at English headquarters in an official international for 17 years. More important, the victory laid the foundation for a remarkable season. Scotland was defeated at Swansea by 12 points to nil and then at Ravenhill Park, Belfast, a tremendous struggle was won by Wales by two tries to a penalty goal.

There were amazing scenes of jubilation on the part of Welsh supporters, who had witnessed the first Triple Crown triumph in 39 years, while the reputation of Gwilliam as a leader was secure and 13 Welshmen were included in the British Lions tour of New Zealand and Australia.

The fourth and final match of the season against France at Cardiff completed the grand slam with a 21-0 victory. The Welsh team had to fight hard in the first half against a determined French side and it was only the absence of Jean Prat through injury, in the second half, that enabled Wales to cut loose and win comfortably. Yet it ended an outstanding season, which delighted Welshmen and completed a change in the approach to international rugby which had been launched successfully by Ireland in 1948 and continued by them in 1949.

It was termed 'Triple Crown' rugby and, for the first time in the British Isles, forwards were made the spearhead rather than the backs. In actual fact, it was the establishment of a style of play which is now called 'second-phase' rugby, since mobile, aggressive, forward-moving packs established a supremacy by dominating in the set pieces and loose play, harassing the opposing half-backs, committing defenders, and then restarting their own attacks from the breakdowns or tackles in the loose.

The style was not readily accepted by the purists who did not appreciate that it would soon become the basic pattern of play—it is now, of course, the only way to succeeed in representative rugby. Thus to Ireland and Wales must go the credit for this new approach, although British sides are still far behind Southern Hemisphere countries in the perfection of the technique. However, physical size and power plays a more important part nowadays at forward than ever before. A simple indication of the growth and development of forwards is revealed by the comparison of the average weights of New Zealand packs in 1905 (12 st. 7 lb.) and 1969 (16 st.).

The leader of this Welsh side, John Gwilliam, was a

shrewd student of rugby football and its players when he took over command of the national XV, a few hours before the England match. He had played at Cambridge and served in the Army and was mature at 26 years of age with an amusing, optimistic sense of humour that enabled him to lead and discipline his side in a new way, since one felt he was never involved, emotionally, in the proceedings. Gwilliam was an unusual Welsh captain; but he earned the respect of his men, who obeyed him on the field of play, even though several senior players did not, always, agree with him in principle! He was a true captain and whenever things went wrong he accepted the blame readily, as during the Scottish debacle at Murrayfield in 1951, when his 'team of all the talents' were humbled 19-0.

Yet despite the temporary falling away in 1951, Gwilliam and his team returned to power in 1952, and proved themselves—what I still consider them to be—the strongest Welsh team of the post-War years. Gwilliam says of the 1950 Welsh team, 'The real basis of the side's success was due to the fact that we had a collection of young, talented and enthusiastic players. There was a nucleus of experienced campaigners of the calibre of Matthews, Cleaver and Jones, but they were not blasé and everyone in the side was keen to win. They were "competitive" players in the best sense of that word.'

He goes on to say that although there were many gifted players in the side it is difficult to single out individual members. Cliff Davies was a member of an outstanding Cardiff team, and as Gwilliam said, 'He was accustomed to winning and expected to win at international level, while Roy John and Ray Cale were comparatively unknown until they played at Twickenham but then revealed how forwards could dominate a game. R. T. Evans will be remembered for his devastating tackling, while D. M. Davies became a leading exponent in the art of hooking.'

Gwilliams's basic pattern of approach was simple and clear cut, 'Always we aimed to encamp in our opponents' half;

always we aimed to win the ball cleanly when our forwards were going forward. There was no discipline in a military sense, of course, but if anyone failed to tackle he was reminded of it! In general, the standard of play was attained by continual encouragement and exhortation during the game. Naturally, we were very interested in the game itself and noted the methods of other teams and the skills of their individuals. We played with the object of using the ability of our team to the best advantage.'

Gwilliam declares there are three basic qualities for the achievement of success in representative rugby, as follows: (1) Brilliant, or fortunate, selectors; (2) A careful study of the game so that no situation in any match can arise which has not previously been considered by the captain; and (3) To extract every ounce of skill and energy from 15 players at the same time, and to produce the willingness and enthusiasm of all of them to support the defence and attack, and to maintain team spirit off the field.

The 1950 and 1952 Welsh sides achieved this and hold high places in the honours list.

The 1951-52 Springboks

Whenever one is asked as to which touring team in the British Isles since the War proved the most impressive, one is always tempted to nominate the 1951-52 Springboks. There are special reasons for this, and an important one in my case is the fact that as a high school player I was deeply impressed by the 1931-32 Springboks led by Bennie Osler. At that age one tends to watch the top-class players closely and study their style, and even attempt to imitate them, albeit not too successfully. I can recall being fascinated by the accuracy of Osler's kicking. Again, one of his two scrum-halves, a young theological student, Danie Craven, also caught the eye.

Against Neath and Aberavon, the referee had the temerity

to advise Craven on how the ball should be put into the scrum. This was quite sensational and even my predecessor on the *Western Mail*, rather unkindly I thought at the time, accused Craven of 'sharp practice'. In fact, the referee and the critic had both disregarded the power to the first shove by the most powerful Springbok pack ever to visit these shores. I watched them in action several times and kept all the cuttings of their tour, as high school boys still tend to do. I collected autographs, as well, and still treasure them!

The next Springbok side I watched in action was that of twenty years later. By that time I was a critic and met them in London. At the Press conference, when I mentioned the *Western Mail*, the assistant manager Danie Craven smiled and remarked, 'Your paper once called me a cheat!' When I replied, 'Yes I know, and I saw the match!', it was the start of a close friendship in the game. Of all managements, at home and abroad, only one pair has equalled Frank Mellish and Danie Craven, and they were Siggins and Davies of the 1955 Lions. Perhaps it was that both pairs were fortunate that the 1950's were such vintage years for good players and teams; the last great days before the strictly disciplined pattern play. The 1951-52 Springboks were successful in many ways, and not least because of the excellent management.

This is what the side's captain has to say of his management: 'When South Africa appoints two Springboks as manager and assistant, the team always seems to do better. The 1951-52 side had two Springboks to guide and lead them; one jovial and almost liberal, and the other one stern, strict and conservative in his outlook, and these two blended in perfect combination.' A shrewd comment this, for Frank Mellish would smoke and smoke during a match, perhaps a dozen cigarettes as well as taking a few quick nips from a pocket flask. Danie Craven would watch, intently, without smoking and certainly not drinking. One was jovial and liberal and one strict and conservative but, as Kenyon says, what a perfect combination. Yet the captain, too, did an outstanding job in a special way.

Basil Kenyon, as Gilbert and Sullivan would say, was 'a jolly good captain', too! He led the side with a friendly discipline after suffering a serious eye injury in the third match at Pontypool. As he himself said, the injury acted as tremendous motivation for the players to please him. Hennie Muller, the superb No. 8 forward, was the vice-captain and deputised most ably for Kenyon in the international matches.

Yet the outstanding quality of this perfectly balanced side, blessed with all the text-book qualities, was its team spirit. Kenyon believes it to be 'the best in the history of the game in South Africa'. Craven agrees for, as the most devoted disciple of Springbok rugby, he has the 1951 side very close to his heart. They are still his 'favourites' although he played in what was, perhaps, the greatest of Springbok sides, that which toured Australia in 1937. When you talk to the 'maestro' about the tour of 1951-52 his eyes light up and his face beams, for he cannot hide his genuine love for this particular side.

I got to know the party really well and the tour was a happy, exciting experience, free from controversial incident, from the moment Peter Cooper penalised them at the first scrum in their first match at Bournemouth, to the final whistle of the Barbarians match at Cardiff.

They played 31 matches, won 30 and lost one; scoring 62 points against 167. They had a tremendous battle with Cardiff, with Wales at Cardiff against the Triple Crown side and were beaten only by the London Counties who rose magnificently to the occasion at Twickenham.

The behaviour of the players was an important factor in their success for they had a strict code towards good manners which included the meeting of strangers. No Springbok side has ever mixed as well, before or since, as did these fellows, and when they presented the Springbok head to Cardiff at the end of the tour in a crowded club room, because they felt they were 'morally beaten' by the Club, they made enough friends in that hour of sportsmanship to last them a lifetime.

As one of few outsiders privileged to attend a Springbok reunion in South Africa, I can vouch for the fact that the 1951 friendships are very real and lasting.

They approached the game wisely, practised and planned, and knew all about second-phase rugby. As Kenyon explains: 'The main emphasis in our planning was that our opponents had to be forced to play our game, which meant that they could not play theirs, and thus half the battle was won that way. As France produced a different pattern they were closely studied, and Craven and I went up to Edinburgh to watch them play against Scotland. At the match we worked out our tactics against France and incorporated them in our planning.

'Briefly, our pattern was this— Tight play was never to be neglected but to form the basis for second-phase attack which we knew we could win, possessing the speed to do so among the loose forwards. Once the loose forwards mastered the ball, they brought the tight forwards back into play, hence the many passing movements among the forwards. When the loose forwards were forced to form a loose scrum, the ball went out to the backs who had to round off the movement. Therefore, tight play to soften up our opponents, loose play to send backs away or bring forwards back into play.

'From our own possession our backs could find the openings. If they took the outside gap, the wings went over or, if the inside gap, the forwards carried on the movement. If they were tackled, the loose scrum or loose maul saw to it that the ball was kept alive for our attack.'

When asked whether the Springboks were disciplined in their pattern of play, Kenyon replied, 'It was necessary to dictate the pattern of play if the recognised pattern was not followed. It often happened that our forwards became too loose, and the line-outs were used to bring them closely together into a unit. Backs, perhaps, kicked too much or did not use their line enough, but those were all subsidiaries in the major pattern.'

Craven says of Kenyon, 'He was the most unlucky but the

greatest of Springbok captains, while Muller's heart was always bleeding for his boys!'. Prop Chris Koch was the biltong king; wing Buks Marais was the first Springbok to buy a bowler hat; the bald-headed flanker Basie Van Wyk 'threw the bones'; Salty du Rand, a fine lock, sang lustily, and Basie Viviers was a useful utility player and an outstanding touch judge with a cloth cap, who later became the 1956 Springbok captain.

Half-backs Hannes Brewis and Fonnie du Toit were durable, shrewd and effective; Jaap Bekker was a powerful prop and another prop, 'veteran' Okey Geffin, proved an amazingly accurate medium-range place-kicker. Full-back Johnny Buchler was courageous while the powerful wrestler Gert Dannhauser was the gentlest of men. One could go on about this side, for all its members were interesting individuals yet devotedly together as a team. If for no other match than the victory against Scotland at Murrayfield, they will be remembered. This game was won by 44 points to nil and as a disappointed Scot remarked after the final whistle, 'We were lucky to get the nought!'. The Springboks were brilliant that day; scoring nine tries and no penalty goals; they were probably as great a force as any team in rugby history. They were an outstanding side. They had it all!

The 1955 British Lions

If I had to say which was the most enjoyable side I have watched over a period, without hesitation I would answer, hand on heart, 'The 1955 British Lions'. This does not mean, necessarily, that it was the most efficient or ruthlessly successful, but the most fascinating and the one that shared in the most attractive and exciting Test match series of all time.

Many factors could have combined to direct my judgment, such as it is, in this assessment, for the 1955 tour was the first long one I had the privilege to make. Again, the team was the happiest one I have ever known. The management were close friends; I shared this trip with an intrepid correspondent, and South Africa was then, and remains, a truly remarkable and fascinating country. Yet now with the experience of five successive Lions tours, and the many tours within the British Isles, I still regard 1955 as the brightest year of the Lions and the one side that held the attention throughout.

Even when they were losing by 20 points to nil at Port Elizabeth, with the flame-haired O'Reilly at full-back, and Robin Roe playing hooker with a corset worn beneath his jersey to hold damaged ribs together, they were still a special side. In defeat their brightly shining star could not be dimmed. They were, as John Reed would modestly remark— 'The Greatest!'

Fifteen years later—how time flies members of the team still enjoy meeting and the light of battle reveals itself in their eyes when they talk of the Tests and the special victories, none perhaps greater than at Kroonstad, the Llanelli of South African rugby. Again, when the scarlet-jerseyed warriors meet those who, with equal pride and success, wore the green jerseys of South Africa, the handshakes are strong and warm and the admiration and respect for each other equally sincere. It was a Test series without incident and the first of the four matches remains the greatest ever played.

One does not use this superlative casually, for August 6, 1955 produced the 'cliff-hanger' of all time with a final score of 23-22, and South Africa just failing to make it 24-23 with the last kick of the match. How wrong it would be to remember this Homeric struggle between rugby giants only because Jack Van der Schyff, said to have been a crocodile hunter in his spare time, missed the last vital kick. He had kicked four goals previously and played well. It was not his fault, since the Lions scored five tries to four and played through the second half with 14 men and seven forwards. It was a match that had to be won by them, for it was the accolade by which they will be remembered and, as a mere rugby writer, I am proud to record that 'I was there!'

Recently, I persuaded a friend and colleague in the 'trade'; one who was in the centre of this illustrious side, for he was something more than a great player, the 'radio-active particle' around which the whole social side of the happy team revolved, to write down what he thought to be the reasons why it was an outstanding side, so that I could compare them with my own. After 15 years, Cliff Morgan's reasons and findings were still almost identical to my own!

Morgan believes, as I do, that the 1955 Lions were a side of exceptional natural talent that was exploited to the full, although this could have been the team's greatest strength as well as its greatest weakness. It had two players of Test standard for almost every position, except perhaps at full-back where illness and injury hit both Angus Cameron and Alun Thomas. Its tight forwards were genuine ones whose primary task at all times was to win the ball, and they continued in their industry throughout the tour, knowing that the possession they won would be well used and, generally, it was!

The front row was strong enough to hold the Springboks, Koch, Van der Merwe and Bekker, and won a half share of the ball, while the second row jumped well; held its own at the line-out and did its bit in the tight. The back row were destructive but also creative, and the eight were a unit, knowing what they were doing and working in close co-ordination with the backs. The inside backs were quick and accurate in attack and defence, creating opportunities, and the threequarters well able to run at, and away from, the opposition.

As Morgan said: 'We simply played the basics. We needed the ball and the forwards got stuck in and got it. We had a theory that there is no such thing as a bad ball. Any ball is good if you have players who are capable of something out of the ordinary. The team did have an awareness of the essential difference between strategy and tactics. Our strategy was to run the ball and in so doing make the opposition chase us. The kick was not to be used to get out of trouble, but to put ourselves in a situation to attack. Having watched the Springboks play, we decided not to waste all our forwards' energy in a test of physical strength. We had the notion that we could not tire out superb Springbok fitness by kicking down field, for they could run all day; but we suspected that they could not turn quickly. The aim therefore was to retain possession and switch direction as much as possible. However, we did study the opposition to note their strength and weaknesses, while Jeff Butterfield could 'read' a game so well. His direction in the Free State match was uncanny.'

However, Morgan believes that a weakness of the 1955 side was that they played it, for the most part, off the top of their heads! He adds, 'Would that we had had a coach to string together the available gifts. It may then have been a truly great side.' Modesty forbids Morgan to say that it was a great side and its try-scoring record per match was the best of any Lions' team in South Africa with 94 tries in 24 matches. Many of these tries were superb, and Butterfield, Morgan, O'Reilly, Johnny Williams and Bryn Meredith scored some sparkling ones. These I will remember always, as well as the modest smiles of the party. They knew they were good, but they never said so, and throughout the tour it was one for all and all for one, with managers Siggins and Davies applying a 'touch of the tiller' when needed.

Oxford University, 1955

By far the most unusual and, perhaps, fascinating of the outstanding post-War sides was that developed and prepared by Oxford University during the Michaelmas term, towards the end of 1955. During this short period, which contained 12 matches including the all-important one against Cambridge University at Twickenham, Oxford University captured the sporting headlines with a remarkable exhibition of 'way-out' rugby that deceived many yet proved immensely successful. It was never fully approved at the time by the establishment of the game, and I confess to having doubts myself, but in the light of what has happened in the past 15 years this side, captained by Durban born South African R. C. P. Allaway, was the pathfinder. Following in its wake, a dozen years later, came organised coaching, squad training and dedication, and the 'dedication' and discipline of Oxford in 1955 is now much more commonplace than it was then, and the place of the running scrum-half and the linking with back-row forwards is an essential feature of the modern game.

Allaway was elected captain in his third year, having played in the two previous inter-Varsity matches, and was a shrewd, intelligent, imaginative psychologist in his approach to his team and the game. He had eight old Blues in residence with him and one remarkable freshman in D. O. Brace, a dashing, diminutive 22-year-old Welshman, who had distinguished himself as captain of the Welsh Secondary Schools, and who had already played two seasons apiece with Aberavon and Newport. A running, elusive, quick-thinking scrum-half, he found a friend indeed in Allaway, and they combined closely and easily to engineer the driving force of what has been quite the most entertaining Oxford side in the post-War years.

Aiding and abetting them were M. J. K. Smith, at outside-half, who had previously played twice at full-back and established himself as a cricketer of great promise; two strong centres in Reeler and Fallon, and a particularly powerful pack by University standards. Only two of the pack were new 'blues' and one of these, R. H. Davies on the flank, was to play again in 1956 and 1957 and gain his first Welsh cap in the following season. John Currie and Peter Robbins moved into the England side after the inter-Varsity match to become outstanding players.

The side lost its first match against Richmond at Iffley

Road, as Allaway was in the process of sorting out the available resources, but from that match onwards they raged like a prairie fire across England and Wales and every rugby student and theorist went to see them and either talk or write about them. Many went into ecstacies at the intricate skills displayed; some delayed their decision, while others were most critical. The criticism and comment did not worry Allaway and his fellows, but the enthusiasm for the team on the part of spectators cheered its members as they won match after match and defeated Gloucester 11-6, Cardiff 23-6, Blackheath 20-9, Harlequins 17-3, London Scottish 3-0 and shared a draw with a strong Stanley's XV 21-21, which was probably the best match of the term. As the term developed, so the side improved and Brace has one word for it, 'togetherness', which made the team a 'family'. The side was above average in intelligence and more mature than most university sides. Its members obtained good degrees and Allaway himself got a 2 (1) in Law while Brace was already a graduate of University College, Cardiff.

As Brace pointed out, recently, in a fascinating discussion about the side—for this special experience stands out vividly in his memory—'It was quite the happiest and most exciting period of my playing career. The team spirit, enthusiasm and dedication was quite tremendous, while Allaway was an outstanding leader. It was a revelation to experience the effort and thought that went into each match. The preparations were exacting and nothing was left undone. In many ways our matches were won during the thorough training sessions, for every afternoon, except on match days and Sundays, we worked really hard under the direction of Allaway, and every manoeuvre in the open and set piece was done over and over again until it was perfect. The 'switch' and its variations were practised, although it often appeared to the onlooker at a match that it was something produced on the spur of the moment. Individualism was not subdued, but fitted into the whole approach of the team, and we developed a concise but accurate code of signals which were never 'broken' by our opponents.'

The training sessions started with a team talk in the pavilion when the happenings in the previous match were analysed. A magnetic blackboard was employed and each player was allowed to have his say, while every player grew to appreciate what was required of the other positions on the field. The discussion session lasted for half an hour and a squad of 20 players took part. This was followed by 45 minutes of physical activities on the field. Everyone trained in spikes and the forwards were speeded up while every effort was made to improve their handling because the intricate switches required accurate handling by all players.

The constant handling in these sessions improved the confidence of all concerned and a third session was devoted to backs in one half of the field and forwards in the other. Each group practised with dedication and special attention was paid to throwing in from touch and the use of signals. The forwards scrummaged against a college pack and also used a scrummaging machine, in what was the most dedicated post-War term at Oxford. The whole session ended with a period of 'ghost' rugby and then a couple of tackles per man against the 'bag'.

It was exacting but produced a remarkably high standard of fitness, and the feeling of 'togetherness', which Brace highlights, was the vital secret of the side's success. The senior players in the side, like Currie and Robbins, provided invaluable knowledge and advice during the term, while Allaway made each player believe in himself and the side. Clubs attempted to combat the Oxford manoeuvres, but often got themselves into difficulties while so doing. It was interesting to hear Brace say that there was discussion before the playing of Stanley's match, at which Cambridge representatives are always present, as to whether Oxford should reveal their whole repertoire of manoeuvres, and eventually it was decided to do so, since it was felt that this might confuse Cambridge, who would have comparatively little time to devise counter methods. As Clement admitted after the

'Varsity match, the Oxford intentions proved worthwhile and snatched the initiative, if ever there is one before the start in this important match!

Oxford studied the opposition closely before each match and adjusted their tactics accordingly to meet the strength of the opposition. Against the bigger, stronger packs, the Oxford backs demanded 40 per cent of the possession from the set pieces and as much as possible from the loose. Again, Oxford attempted to retain possession as long as possible and this tired as well as confused their opponents.

The *Playfair Rugby Annual* described the approach as follows: 'The essential idea would seem to be a puzzling change of direction in attack so far as possible from the encircling spoilers and other defenders. This sometimes led to the scrum-half running backwards some yards to link up with his fellows. As many as two or three scissors-like exchanges of the ball might follow in the hope of throwing the defence well on to the wrong foot, and even standing still wondering which way to move. Against Cambridge, this deliberate sacrifice of ground in opening an attack did succeed more than once in puzzling the defence.'

Oxford won the Varsity match and defeated a good Cambridge side that contained eight players who were either capped or to be capped, including Arthur Smith, R. W. D. Marques, W. R. Evans, T. B. Richards and J. G. Hetherington. Cambridge scored first through Kershaw with Hetherington combining as a result of an Oxford error in launching a counter attack, but the Dark Blues did not deviate from their original intentions and their approach carried the day in the end.

Brace increased his efforts to force attacks and several times Cambridge were hard pressed in defence, wondering whether Oxford had more than fifteen players on the field! A clever switch put Smith through and he kicked over Hetherington's head, only to be obstructed, and Currie kicked the penalty goal. Thus it was 5-3 to Cambridge at the interval, but Oxford soon took the lead when Reeler burst through after gathering a dropped pass and put Walker over Another try came when Brace and Smith launched yet one more attack. Again Smith kicked ahead for Fallon to put Reeler over for the decisive try and it was Oxford who called the tune until the end.

They left the field happy men, for it was an excellent match following three bad years. Both captains had met and discussed ways and means of lifting the annual fixture out of the 'slough of despond'. They did so, splendidly, and Oxford became the most talked about side for many, many years. They set people thinking and talking everywhere, and their dedicated approach is now employed by many sides and even countries. For this they deserve all praise!

England, 1957

Had not Keith Maddocks of Neath, making his only appearance for Wales, at Cardiff on January 19, 1957, been a little slow in getting back to an on-side position while a line-out was taking place on the other side of the field inside the Welsh half, England would not have won the Triple Crown or achieved the 'Grand Slam' so deservedly in the 1956-57 season. His casual and unintentional default was spotted by an alert referee, Mr. A. I. Dickie of Scotland, in the first half of the match and he awarded, quite correctly, a penalty to England which full-back, D. F. Allison, had no difficulty in converting. Thus a match that was never inspiring or really exciting was won by England by a penalty goal to nil, as it was the only score, though the Welsh full-back, T. J. Davies, just failed with a long-range attempt that would have earned a draw.

However, the match was remarkable for two reasons. It was the first occasion after World War II Wales took the field without K. J. Jones, who had played in all the 43 official

England 1957. The England captain Eric Evans presents his side to the Duke of Edinburgh. Players *(l to r)*: Evans, Hastings, Jacobs, Jeeps and Bartlett.

Wales. 1969. *Standing (l to r):* D. P. D'Arcy (referee), S. J. Watkins, W. D. Thomas, T. M. Davies, B. Thomas, D. Williams, W. D. Morris, D. J. Lloyd, F. B. Stephens (touch judge). *Sitting:* D. C. T. Rowlands (coach), J. P. R. Williams, J. Young, G. O. Edwards (capt.), K. S. Jarrett, M. C. R. Richards. *In front:* S. J. Dawes, J. Taylor, B. John.

Maurice Richards of Cardiff and Wales. The outstanding player of 1969.

matches since the resumption—Maddocks was only the second right-wing to appear for Wales in ten seasons! Jones was then 35 years of age and was to play in one more match, the next against Scotland, which was his last appearance after a long and colourful career in the scarlet jerseys of Wales and the British Isles. He scored 17 tries in 44 appearances for Wales and 16 tries in as many appearances for the Lions!

Secondly, England, having just cleared the first hurdle at the Cardiff Arms Park, their third win at the ground in four visits, went on to develop into a sound side of all-round ability that won the Triple Crown and the Championship, under the virile leadership of Eric Evans, to give the 1950 British Lions' manager, Surgeon-Rear Admiral L. B. 'Ginger' Osborne, a happy year of office as President of the RFU!

Eric Evans was a remarkable leader in many ways and, even before the season started, had made 21 appearances; he finished his career eventually, as England's most-capped hooker at the end of the next season, during which he was captain and again led England to the top of the table. Thus he ended only one cap behind the record-holder of the time, Lord Wakefield, whom D. P. Rogers surpassed in 1969. Evans was as tough as teak as a player, voluble, durable, domineering and shrewd. His flow of language was colourful, though never malicious, and the late John Daniell would have been hard pressed as a rival pack-leader, in this respect, to match the sandy-haired, slightly bow-legged Evans.

He generated drive, discipline and enthusiasm and these are three important ingredients for any successful side. Evans says that the England team's success in 1957 was based upon the fundamentals and team spirit. The side possessed several outstanding players and the following members were 1955 Lions—J. Butterfield, W. P. C. Davies, R. E. G. Jeeps, A. Ashcroft and A. R. Higgins, while R. W. D. Marques and P. B. Jackson were honoured in 1959. The side possessed a strong workmanlike pack that played as a unit and the number of caps received individually by the eight before they eventually retired are as follows: Jacobs 29, Evans 30,

Hastings 13, Marques 23, Currie 25, Ashcroft 16, Robbins 19 and Higgins 13. Among the leading backs there were Jackson 20, Butterfield 28, Thompson 17, Davies 11, Bartlett 7 and Jeeps 24. Thus this side had experience and potential and it arrived in the middle of a settled period of selection, which is always an advantage in any country. When a group of good players, and possibly some brilliant ones, are together in a national side for a number of seasons, a strong sense of team work and confidence is produced, and this was in a period long before the days of the national training squad and intensive coaching. The captain was the coach and he, and the chairman of selectors, devised the plan of campaign.

The real strength of the side was in Evans as hooker, Marques and Currie in the second row, Robbins as a spoiler and Ashcroft as a coverer, Jeeps as a sturdy scrum-half, Bartlett as a link outside-half, and Butterfield and Davies as an ideal centre-pair. The last two had been outstanding in South Africa in 1955, with Butterfield elusive and subtle and Davies strong and thrusting. England has not fielded a better team since in the post-War years, though having a good one in 1963.

There was much individual skill in the side and, as Evans says, 'Individual skill can always be used providing it does not sacrifice the efficiency of the whole team simply to demonstrate the extent of individual ability.' This is what the national coaches, quite rightly, are preaching now, and thus the shrewd Evans was on the right lines in those days.

His basic pattern was really common-sense; to win the game at forward, starting with the front row. Opponents were studied but Evans believed that if you have accurate co-ordination and your team is good enough, any opposing side can be mastered, although he feels 'it is a distinct advantage to know the strength and weaknesses of those against you'.

Of his side's approach, he says, 'Ours was a disciplined approach, very definitely, and perhaps being mature in the game I was able to enforce discipline. I received every encouragement from the Chairman of Selectors, Carson

Catcheside, and I am myself a great believer in strong discipline.'

Of his own skill, he says, 'As far as that was concerned I thought I was adequate. I went to a lot of trouble to get and keep extremely fit, and achieve an above average pack leader loud voice but, above all, I think I had the respect of the team members, who were prepared to help whatever deficiences I might have had.' Here, Evans was speaking honestly, for he is now a selector, and tries to maintain such standards in the teams he helps to pick each season. He was dedicated and, if a 'character' off the field, he allowed the wise-cracking to hide the true determination of a North-countryman to win!

When discussing the qualities of a good side, Evans is quick to point out that such a side on the field must be good friends off it. The need for confidence and trust in one another is vital and, above all, to have trust and respect for the captain. Evans appreciates that he had a good side to lead but, in all modesty, argues that a good side must have an efficient captain. He feels that a captain's influence is vital and that sound team spirit can only be developed over a period.

After beating Wales in 1957, England travelled to Dublin where they were successful by a try and a penalty goal to nil before moving back to Twickenham to beat a strong French side in a hard match by three tries to a goal. This left only Scotland and they were beaten at Twickenham, more than comfortably, by two goals, one penalty and a try to a penalty. By this match England had settled into a fine combination and would have gone on improving had there been more matches to play.

In the next season England beat the touring Wallabies and remained unbeaten in the championship but could only draw with Wales and Scotland. Some of the trouble was at outside-half where Horrocks-Taylor at first, and then a recalled Bartlett, never gave quite enough punch to the mid-field in order to exploit the powerful threequarter line. Still, the winning of the championship in two successive seasons is a rare achievement, and this England side did it under Evans. However, the 1957 side was the stronger unit and one of the best fielded by England in the post-War years, if not *the* best.

The 1959 British Lions

The British side managed by the Scot, A. W. Wilson, and captained by the Irishman, A. R. Dawson, was a much better side than its record suggests, although this in itself was more than useful, with 27 victories in 33 matches and the massive total of 842 points, the highest achieved by a British touring team. Following its daily activities was a most exciting and pleasant task, and although at the time one both praised and criticised it, I do feel now that I may have criticised more severely than was necessary. In view of what has happened since, and especially in New Zealand, this 1959 side was a remarkably good one with an excellent record.

It should have shared, at least, the Test series with New Zealand, for in only one of the four matches was it truly beaten—the third at Christchurch—and during the tour a British team first experienced the special interpretation of the laws which has become peculiar to the land. Fortunately, during the tour, the International Board met in New Zealand and some of the discrepancies were removed, although some still remain.

Dawson suggests, correctly I feel, that the success was based on an extremely happy touring party, which contained a considerable amount of individual talent and natural rugby ability, and whose members had a reasonable understanding of what was required to succeed in New Zealand. He adds, 'Allied to these points was a considerable amount of dedication and willingness to work hard, plus an endless supply of courage.'

He makes an interesting point, one that is true of all touring teams visiting New Zealand, 'We were well aware in theory of the tremendous dedication and power forward play in New Zealand, but had no real conviction of this until we had experienced it. Our forward play was true to form in the British Isles at that time, and in fact as it still is today—loose, without principle—which affected the quality of the possession given to the backs; and having had a relatively easy first section of the tour in Australia, we realised quickly how poor our forward play was, having played one or two games in New Zealand.

'I think that this realisation that we had much work to do, and the spirit with which the team applied themselves to the task, was the real basis of success.' As Dawson was the side's captain and hooker in all six tests, he could appreciate better than most the rapid improvement made by his forwards and how they battled through to finish the tour on an exceptionally high note by winning the fourth and final Test, in New Zealand, after being robbed of the first and almost winning the second. Only in the third Test were they decisively beaten, and their showing was the best by a post-War touring team in New Zealand, except for the 1949 Wallabies who excelled when most of the leading All Blacks were in South Africa.

Dawson agreed that the forwards did a tremendous job both in provincial matches and the Tests, except for the third Test at Christchurch, when the All Blacks were at their superb best. Danie Craven, watching the match, paid them the compliment of saying, 'You could have covered the New Zealand pack with a blanket throughout the game!' Dawson singles out the three big, tight forwards, R. H. Williams, W. R. Evans and W. A. Mulcahy, for their efforts, saying, 'they were tireless in their work for possession of the ball'. Again, the set scrummaging was equal to the task of obtaining a half-share of possession and the back row was fast enough to contest possession from broken play. G. K. Smith, J. W.

Faull, N. A. A. Murphy and H. J. Morgan excelled in the vigorous loose play.

The management, wisely I feel, committed the team to an attacking approach, for the back division contained some truly brilliant runners, but it would not have been possible without the gallant work of the forwards. It was felt that to attempt to engage New Zealand purely at forward in their own country was another form of suicide. It was thus decided that the attack should be based on 'first principles by obtaining possession, making ground, and following by change of direction and support at speed'.

The side contained the players to do this for R. E. G. Jeeps and A. A. Mulligan were sound at scrum-half; Risman at outside-half possessed the special ability of being able to dictate a game, and there were competent players in midfield, with one a player of genius in D. Hewitt, and two outstanding wings in P. B. Jackson and A. J. F. O'Reilly. I would go so far as to state that these two were the best PAIR of wings ever to appear in a Lions' side—and, indeed, almost any other side. The full-backs, T. J. Davies and K. J. F. Scotland, were players of exceptional ability in contrasting style. Davies was powerful and Scotland elusive, and the joining of attacks by Scotland was a feature of the side's approach.

It is fair to suggest that Scotland was the forerunner of the attacking full-back required by the present no touch-kicking dispensation law, while Davies was an answer to Don Clarke as a rush-stopper, tackler and place-kicker; it was a tribute to the both of them that they appeared together in the winning Test side, with Scotland revealing his versatility in the centre. The players were individuals but played as a team, for O'Reilly got 17 tries and Jackson 16. Again, like the Springboks of 1951-52, these Lions considered their opponents in detail, and a close study was made of the All Black forwards and their supporting halves. However, as Dawson comments, 'Other than great forward play, there was Don Clarke, who had a terrific influence on New Zealand rugby at the time. The memories of Dunedin and the First

Test are sufficient evidence of this!'

Dawson led the Lions and Whineray the All Blacks. The Irishman says of his friendly rival, 'Whineray, in my opinion, became one of the great international rugby captains of modern times. In 1959 he was influenced, perhaps, by "the system" and, perhaps, his coach and the All Blacks were rather confused by the changes of direction and speed of our players, but the Test results proved their ability at dealing with these variations.'

The Lions held meetings and discussions and there was much pre-match planning. Dawson was a conscientious captain; Wilson was a determined manager, and Glasgow a cheerful assistant manager. I got to know them well during the five months tour and they treated Vivian Jenkins and myself with courtesy and generosity. Sometimes we disagreed, but we always 'agreed to disagree' without any bad feeling. There were very few 'incidents' on tour, and the Lions were a happy party with a particularly high standard of intelligence. There were 'clowns' like Ray Prosser and Alan Ashcroft but they were no fools, as their clowning hid a shrewdness and friendliness plus determination as players. Again, O'Reilly, Mulligan and Marques with their slick 'That was the week that was' banter (long before the programme was thought of) would have destroyed many managers, but Alf Wilson survived, not only to return to New Zealand in 1966, but to become an important figure in world rugby!

This team of much talent was full of personalities; more than in any side I have known, even more than the more successful 1955 side, and the two sides (1955 and 1959) must be regarded as the best Lions of the Century. Dawson, with due modesty says, 'Captaincy, therefore, on the field, became a matter of implementing the normally accepted duties and it is always relatively easy to captain a good team.' It is a tribute to this side that it finished the tour with some of its best performances against strong opposition. The matches at Rotorua and Whangarei were tremendous and the final Test win clinched for the 1959 Lions the title of the best all-round side to visit New Zealand since World War II. They played well and enjoyed playing, and they broke records everywhere. They had plenty of 'umph'. They were attractive to watch. They scored tries. They hit the headlines the right way, as did the 1955 side. They earned the acclamation of all.

London Welsh, 1967-68

The rage of London club rugby for the past five seasons has been the London Welsh under the captaincy of John Dawes. He took over the leadership at the start of the 1965-66 season and inspired the club to produce effective, running rugby and establish itself as the top club in the Metropolitan area. He accepted his sixth successive season of captaincy for 1970 71 and thus created a record for his own club and probably an achievement that has not been equalled on many occasions in any British club.

In 1967-68 season, which was probably their best of their long run achieved during the captaincy of Dawes, they won the *Sunday Telegraph* Pennant for the best club in England and were second to Llanelli in the Welsh Championship table, while they also won the Middlesex Seven-a-side tournament. The London Welsh had always been a good side, prior to Dawes becoming its captain, but he gathered around him the existing players of merit while others were attracted to the club to form a remarkable unit. The full record for the season was 36 matches played, 25 won, three drawn, eight lost and they scored 579 points with 320 against. The matches lost were against Cardiff, Llanelli (2), Neath, Abertillery, Northampton, Bedford and Pontypool. They were strongly challenged on many occasions and among their more spectacular successes at Old Deer Park were victories over Cardiff (14-6), Neath (45-3) and Newport (17-9 and

22-14), while their leading London rivals, the Scottish, were defeated at the Richmond Athletic Ground (35-9).

Such spectacular and successful rugby caused the turn-stiles at Old Deer Park to click merrily and achieve for the club the best spectator-support in its history, while a shrewd and hard-working committee saw to it that every advantage was taken of the success in rebuilding its facilities and ensuring a happy future. The real basis of the side's success was, as John Dawes says, 'A general footballing ability throughout the side which was necessary for success because you cannot teach this, but you can teach players to scrummage, jump in the line-out, and ruck. Secondly, we tried at all times to attain a New Zealand standard of fitness.'

Individual members of the team played a big part, but first each player had to subject himself to 'team basics', and then his individual skill acted as a bonus for the team. The London Welsh pattern under Dawes has been 'to run with the ball' and to achieve this they always try to play their football on their opponents' side of the 'gain line', irrespective of the actual position on the field of play. Oppposing sides were never studied especially closely, but obviously the 'pre-match build-up' varied in detail with the reputation of their opponents.

The side was always well-disciplined, for as Dawes says, 'In any successful rugby side, discipline is absolutely essential and this can be developed by training and practising together.' However, the side was not always able to dictate the pattern of play, for those few sides who proved stronger 'up front' were able to defeat the London Welsh by playing a tight game, as did Llanelli, who won both matches during the season and pipped the London Welsh for the Welsh club championship title. Of visiting clubs, only Llanelli won at Old Deer Park where the Welsh produced outstanding and consistent rugby.

Against most English opponents the Welsh thoroughly enjoyed themselves and, by the end of each match, the constant running of the Welsh generally got the better of their opponents and tired defences failed to keep them out. The influence of captaincy is important, but Dawes feels that the captain can exert greater influence during training and coaching sessions than on the field of play, although his decisions during matches can make or mar the success of the side. It is true that London Welsh were better prepared than most of their opponents, but even after this special season they did well in 1968-69 because they had, by then, gained an advantage by their three seasons of hard work.

Actually, in 1968-69 they again lost only eight matches and six of these were to Welsh clubs with Cardiff achieving the double and Llanelli a win and a draw. This indicates that the Welsh Championship Table is a fair indication of the relative strength of the four top clubs in position order of Newport, Cardiff, Llanelli and the London Welsh. The big victory of this season was that over Newport at Old Deer Park by 31 points to five, when London Welsh achieved a high peak, while the return match with Newport on Easter Monday was a tremendous affair at Rodney Parade. Wherever the London Welsh played during the four seasons under review, they attracted large crowds and several of their players were honoured by the Welsh selectors. Former club player H. M. Bowcott, who represents the club on the Welsh Rugby Union, was chairman of the national selectors. During this period, former Welsh wing R. W. Boon was the club secretary and he possessed tremendous enthusiasm for the running game. At all times it was a team effort, although the individual players are worthy of praise.

John Dawes, as captain, is deserving of the most praise and was honoured with the captaincy of the Welsh Touring team in the Argentine, followed by a place in the touring team in New Zealand, Australia and Fiji. By the end of 1969-70 he had made 17 appearances for Wales. W. H. Raybould had made seven appearances but moved back to Wales to join Newport in 1969, while John Taylor, a surprise choice for Wales for his first cap against England in 1967, had made 14 appearances by the end of 1970. No. 8 or prop forward R. C. Michaelson had played for Wales in 1963, while I. C. Jones got one cap in 1968 and No. 8 forward T. M. Davies was the most-improved forward in the 1969 national side. Hooker Brian Rees won three caps in 1967 and the young full back, J. P. R. Williams, developed into an outstanding player for club and country in 1969-70.

Never before in their history has the London Welsh produced so many young players for the national fifteen, although in the past more international players had appeared for them than any other club in London. Obviously, there is no reason why any decline should follow this 'Golden Period' and the game has come to expect a high quality of play from the London Welsh at all times. They are contributing much to the game and are always well worth watching. Ymlaen, Cymru Lindain!

Wales 1969

The last outstanding rugby team I watched in action before attempting to write this book of recollections and criticisms, was the championship and Triple Crown side produced by Wales in 1969. Perhaps, because it was Welsh and near to my heart, I was more critical of its development than any other side but once it had revealed itself and achieved a series of impressive performances, one felt it was opportune to praise its virtues which were many and compliment those who shared in the creation of one of the most efficient international sides from the Home Countries for many years.

Despite what the critics of other countries may think, and have often written about myself and my Welsh colleagues, as a rugby nation we are most self-critical and rarely praise Welsh players unless they achieve comparative greatness. It is true that we do not stand by and see our leading players ignored or maligned, especially on tour or against touring teams, but should they play badly or the selectors misuse the

talent available, then we do not spare the rod! The criticism
of our own is often stronger than that made against other
countries, and other teams and players.

This is good, I feel, for it permits a certain amount of
pleasure and satisfaction when things do go right in a good
year! The Welsh never envy others in the game but always
seek to reach the pinnacle themselves. Sometimes they are
slow to adopt new ideas and to discipline their own efforts;
often they disregard young talent without a long enough
trial, for the Welsh are impatient in the game.

The Triple Crown and Championship were won in 1965;
the Championship again in 1966, but then the team fell
away in the years of rebuilding in 1967 and 1968. Many fine
players disappeared from the International scene and the
selectors did not appear to be moving in the right direction.
Some senior players had been discarded too early for lesser
mortals, and coaching had been cast aside by the WRU's
executive as not the answer. Then in June 1968 the Clubs
voiced their opinion at the A.G.M. of the Union and
demanded coaching and a national coach, but this misfired
at first when a Welsh touring team, minus its Lions, gave a
dismal display in the Argentine in the September.

Yet the experience did one man a power of good; for the
hard-headed, shrewd, former captain Clive Rowlands, saw
the possibilities of coaching aided by discipline and team
work. He wanted to establish a band of brothers who would
'die for each other' ... a sort of rugby musketeers idea of
'all for one and one for all'. Wales made him honorary coach
of the national side and carried on with the squad system
devised the previous season by Alun Thomas, Cliff Jones and
Cadfan Davies. He was the catalyst that fused the genius of
the returning British Lions of 1968 with the best of the other
players, and gave just the right aid to an experienced player
as leader, Brian Price of Newport.

Rowlands formula was a simple one ... 'Get the scrummaging right; win good ball in the tight and loose and play
as a team. Look for the ball and use it and support each other

at all times. Give everything you have got but use your
head at all times. 'His technical adviser was Ray Williams,
the WRU's coach organiser, who knew just how much to
organise and how much to leave to Rowlands and Price as
the 'drivers' of men. Time was not on their side, and action
was needed for success.

Two squad training week-ends were arranged at the Afon
Lido at Port Talbot and a squad of 25 players developed a
pattern and a magnificent team spirit. Their confidence in
themselves grew apace and as the season progressed the better
they became. They trusted each other more and more and
became competitors first and foremost, with a plan and a
purpose in their every move. As a team of highly skilled
players they re-emphasised the most important of all rugby
lessons—the team is paramount as a unit; everything must
be directed towards its success.

Against Scotland they were merely warming to their task,
as other nations frowned upon their audacity of 'actually
preparing beforehand' for the encounter. After the first half,
Scotland were never in the hunt, and even in the closing
stages one felt that the Welsh held back, conserving their
energies in the knowledge that they had done more than
enough to succeed.

The Irish burst upon them at Cardiff with traditional fury,
but they were thwarted and their efforts spent against a wall
of unyielding scarlet jerseys. The Welsh were harshly
criticised outside Wales for daring to match the physical
exuberance of the Irish, but they were stronger, better
together and more determined, and by the interval the match
was won. In the second half the play flowed and the genius
of Edwards and John shone brightly with the kicking of
Jarrett and the enthusiasm of the other backs. This was more
promising!

In Paris they met a revitalised French side, inspired by the
magnificent Spanghero, almost as good as themselves and it
was missed kicks at goal that cost them the match, and they
had to be content with a draw. Then came England and

after a stern first half, defensively played into the wind, the rich red wine of success flowed freely in the second half. This was the play of a superbly drilled and efficient team possessing skill, pace and the qualities necessary for success.

Let Brian Price describe why Wales succeeded in 1969: 'It could be said that our success was due to selection of the squad with the recalling of several experienced forwards and blending them with a crop of young and enthusiastic backs. This allied to the spirit induced by the squad training under Clive Rowlands led to a complete understanding of the team policy by every member of the squad. Everyone trained hard and none harder than Norman Gale. The discipline achieved was a result of this approach, while the chance of a tour to New Zealand at the end of the season was the right incentive to do well and made it essential for success to be achieved in the championship of five nations.

'Again I am convinced that only under the controlled squad system can individual talent be exploited. We had an abundance of natural talent. John Williams liked to run at full-back; Gareth Edwards had strength and speed, while Brian Thomas, at the time, was the only forward in the British Isles who could ruck properly, and we fitted all these talents into our overall plan. All the time the other 14 players were trying to set up a situation for the fifteenth to use his particular talent.

'This was the basic plan; to create good ball and run with it. Yet it was not as easy as this, for there was much pre-match planning and preparation. Most important was the method of ensuring good ball in the right place at the right time. Scrummaging was looked at, closely, and practised; various line-out techniques were tried, and switching inside and out by the backs. All these ploys were used to set up good ball situations from which second-phase attacks were launched if needed. We studied opposing sides in some detail, but were more concerned with attack than defence and it was their weaknesses which interested us most.

'A disciplined approach was employed, probably that is

why I was chosen as captain instead of Gareth Edwards, who was younger and out of touch with the older forwards. As captain it was easy to dictate because of the squad system and the developed pattern of play.'

Thus skill and talent is necessary for all top sides, but after watching Wales doing so well one must agree with Price that fitness to a point of ALMOST training professionally is essential, and this combined with disciplined squad training suggests that one cannot fail completely. The need of a captain is still essential for he is the one who must instil confidence and direct the efforts of the individual for the good of the side.

Wales has moved forward a big step in the game, and the other Home Countries must follow for they cannot allow her to continue enjoying the obvious advantage of her new approach. This is why the 1969 side will remain a special one in the history of the game.

Sadly, it was to suffer two major defeats on its tour in the Antipodes by New Zealand in the tests. For all that it achieved in the British Isles, the Welsh pack could not hold the powerful All Blacks eight playing at home. Of course, it could have been different at the Cardiff Arms Park where even France failed to win in 1970! Welshmen hope that the National XV will be really strong when New Zealand visit the Principality again.

PART FOUR

The Players

Cliff Davies

(Bridgend, Kenfig Hill, Cardiff, Barbarians)
Wales and British Lions)

There can be none better loved in Welsh rugby than Cliff Davies, for when he passed away there was hardly a dry eye in the emotional atmosphere of his funeral with the mourners crowded to the doors of the little church. His friends sang beautifully in his memory, and although death is inevitable and mourning universal, only those who were born and lived in the Principality of Wales could feel the true emotion of that day. Clifton Davies, prop-forward, humorist, tourist, friend, husband, father and mine-worker, was a true character of Wales.

When his coffin was borne to its grave by members of the great Cardiff side of 1947-48 and the British Lions side of 1950, a colourful part of Welsh rugby history died prematurely, for Cliff would have sat in the stands of many clubs and stood at the bars of many hostelries, beside his friends and fellow-workers, for many years and regaled all with his stories and his beliefs about life and rugby football.

His manner was gentle and easy, for rarely was he annoyed. He could talk to princes and tramps, affording them the same affection and understanding, and one would always stop to listen to him, while he sang like a true Welshman, from the heart, with a rich voice that possessed melody and charm. Yes, Cliff was a rugby ambassador, in the Home Countries and across the world, and none were more grieved at his death at the age of 46 years than those in authority in New Zealand rugby, where he was a 'character' beloved by all in 1950, touring with the British Lions. Prop forwards are characters, for Graham Budge, Ray Prosser, Sid Millar,

147

Gordon Wood, Snowy White, Stan Bowes, Hughie McLeod and Phil Judd were expert on the field and amusing off it, but Cliff Davies was the greatest 'character' of them all.

He possessed all the good qualities, and the warmth of his personality was infectious. Once he started to chat in any rugby place, he gathered round him listeners, old and young, for his tales were many and he was, especially after his retirement from the field, the Hans Christian Andersen of Welsh rugby. His best tales were about his beloved 'mules', the name given to the Kenfig Hill side, and that club reveres his memory with a magnificent Cliff Davies museum. Famous players from many countries have contributed jerseys, caps and other souvenirs.

He once told me, 'I was fortunate as a youngster in living in a rugby-mad community, who did all they could to encourage up-and-coming youngsters. The secretary of the local side lived at the top of the street and when about 30 of the boys of the village gathered together in the square in front of his sweet shop, he would throw us a football, saying, "Come on, you young mules." It was the encouragement we needed.

'At school my master, H. O. Evans, gave me a book to read on rugby football by the late Gwyn Nicholls, and Evans carried out to the letter the advice of the former Welsh captain while coaching us. I owed a lot to my brother, W. R. "Billy" Davies, who played for Aberavon and Cardiff, and listened to the advice of Welsh Secondary Schools' selector, "Gitto" Davies, while Vernon Eddy helped me considerably when I started playing for Bridgend.'

Up to the start of World War II this was the accepted pattern for the development of young players in the valleys and villages of Wales, but since the War facilities have improved immensely and organised coaching has become part of the general rugby scene.

Davies had many happy and exciting memories, which he enjoyed recalling over a friendly pint of ale while puffing away at his short-stemmed pipe. The Welsh victory at

Twickenham in 1950 and the first Triple Crown triumph in 39 years at Belfast in the same year. Then his tour to New Zealand, and the last Test match at Auckland, when Ken Jones got his special try. But for him the hardest match was that between France and Wales in Paris in 1947. As Davies recalled, 'The French pack of that day was the finest I played against, as it had tremendous weight and skill, as well as speed. For the Welsh forwards to hold them was quite an achievement and the story of Prin-Clary's ear is as famous in Welsh rugby as the War of Jenkins Ear in Spanish history!'

It is almost a legend now that because the Frenchman was interfering with Welsh hooker Billy Gore, prop Davies took a gentle 'nip' of Prin-Clary's ear to calm him down. Yet Davies was the kindest of players and this story could be apocryphal.

Davies always believed the best side in which he played was the Cardiff team of 1947-48 and felt that it was hardly possible for fifteen members of the side to share in so much play in 70 minutes. He said: 'It was a joy to play in that side and even when you were behind, you had a wonderful feeling that any moment someone would do something clever to regain the lead. The players in that side had individual ability, but used it for the benefit of the team and this must be the hallmark of good rugby.' In this Davies is right, for the great sides in history, even though they had outstanding individuals, always played as teams. Never was this more clearly revealed than the Welsh XV of 1969.

When he had his pipe going well, Davies used to enjoy discussing forward play and while he rarely talked about himself as a prototype, since he was the last of the great 'short' props, he used to list the qualities required for the job as follows, 'The art of being a good forward is to acquire a very full knowledge of the game, so that you are able to provide plenty of variety in your play, and be able to adjust your tactics and style as required. Of course, you must be one hundred per cent fit and be able to handle well and control the ball with the feet in wet and dry conditions. Every forward must be a good scrummager or he is of little value to his side, and more than useful at the line-out, since a good service to the backs from set pieces is essential, while in the loose he must seek the ball and keep up with the play at all times.'

All this Davies told me in 1958, and much has happened in the game since then, but the words are still true, and no budding forward can ignore them.

The former playing colleagues and friends in the game of Davies staged a memorial match in his honour at his beloved Cardiff Arms Park in 1968 with Dr. Jack Matthews as the chairman of the organising committee. It was a considerable success and the dependants of this most lovable rugby man and sincere sportsman benefited considerably. It is seldom that the game forgets its great ones; the world will remember, always, Clifton Davies, everyone's friend and an outstanding prop-forward.

B. John and G. O. Edwards

Half-back pairs in Wales go as much together as bacon and eggs or fish and chips and, if they are good, they are every bit as popular and as familiar in the mouths of Welshmen as household words. It is a tradition created by the famous James brothers who appeared for Swansea and Wales at the end of the last century. They were followed by Llewellyn Lloyd and Lou Phillips of Newport, Owen and Jones of Swansea, Bush and David of Cardiff, Delehay and Lewis of Cardiff, Powell and Bowcott of the London Welsh, Tanner and Davies of Swansea, Cleaver and Tanner and Morgan and Willis of Cardiff, and so on until the pairing of John and Edwards of Cardiff.

Wales has always favoured club pairs for the national XV, and appreciated more than other countries the value of the understanding developed at half-back at club level. It is true, of course, that players from separate clubs have also played well together, like Powell and Ralph, Jones and Tanner, Watkins and Rowlands, but it is the club pairs who have survived longest in the Welsh XV, even though Watkins and Rowlands had a successive run of 13 matches during 1963-65. One would not dare to assess which was the greatest of these pairs, as they were often the best of their decade, and one cannot compare, fairly, the qualities for success, which vary from era to era. It suffices to record that most of them enjoyed their moments of greatness against touring teams and in Triple Crown seasons.

The latest colourful pair produced by Wales are the West Walians Barry John and Gareth Owen Edwards, who have appeared together for Cardiff, East Wales, Wales, the Barbarians and the British Lions, and have earned the respect of colleagues, opponents and critics. Injuries have often retarded their progress and number of appearances but they have always bounced back to thrill and entertain because, first and foremost, they enjoy their rugby and are real competitors in the game.

Many times these two modest young men have confided to me, as to how much they enjoy their rugby, win or lose, and how much pleasure the game has given them in the way of travel and the meeting of people. 'Rugby football has provided a new dimension for our lives. We owe it a great deal,' is their comment but they have also given a great deal to the game. In the 1969 international tournament they were in splendid form, whether scoring tries themselves or making them for others, and always playing very much as a unit, although contrasting strongly in their approach.

Edwards is a fierce, dedicated competitor; a tireless, elusive cheeky-chappie at the base of the scrum, playing as if 80 minutes is far too short for him to employ his full repertoire. His energy and shrewd thinking are supported by a tough frame; one made resilient by his interest in and ability at gymnastics. Yet he has suffered many serious injuries and hamstring trouble has plagued him on two overseas tours, often deceiving critics, who have not seen him previously, into believing that he has been overrated by those at home.

However, Edwards has done enough to convince the knowledgeable ones of his true ability, and when he has been compared with the modern 'maestro' Haydn Tanner he has not been flattered, for he has many of the qualities of this magnificent player of immediately before and after World War II. Born in Gwaun-cae-gurwen, the proud son of a miner, he learned his rugby at his local school and then 'graduated' in the game at Millfield School, which has specialised so successfully in producing young sportsmen and women of high quality.

Several Welsh Secondary Schools caps were gained before he entered the Cardiff College of Education to achieve a P.E. diploma and teaching certificate. While there he joined the Cardiff club and forced his way into the 1st XV where he was joined by Barry John, and they developed their special understanding under the watchful eye of coach Roy Bish, a senior P.E. lecturer at Edward's college. John was already a first-class player and international before he migrated from the West to Cardiff, as have so many young backs in recent years, and Llanelli had groomed him for stardom. Their loss was Cardiff's gain.

At Llanelli, John followed in the pattern of his mentor, Carwyn James, a former Llanelli and Wales outside-half and Llandovery coach, who hailed from the same coal-mining village as John, with the picturesque name of Cefneithin. John, without gaining schoolboy honours as did Edwards, revealed an early ability to handle well and kick immaculately, as well as having plenty of time in which to carry out his manoeuvres. Especially was he clever at side-stepping opposing flank-forwards whose main intent was to spoil.

At times one felt he was almost too casual, but his brain was always ice-cool in these early days, and while David Watkins was the reigning monarch in the outside-half position, John was always a future threat to the magical little man from Newport. He was in and out of the Welsh team at first, but untroubled by the twists of fate or criticism received. He seemed to know where he was going in the game and on arrival at Cardiff first played with W. J. Hullin and then with Edwards.

The departure of Watkins to the professional code left John as the new monarch, ready to conquer fresh fields and reveal to the world his consumate skill as a player and a thinker about the game. He and Edwards appeared first together for Wales in November 1967 against New Zealand, and this was the start of what should prove a long and happy association in the scarlet jersey between these two young Welsh-speaking players.

However, their first 'big-time' success came in one week with two further matches against New Zealand for East Wales at Cardiff and the Barbarians at Twickenham, and their performances virtually won them a place on the Lions South African tour of 1968, and rating as the best British pair of their day. The South African tour was spoiled for them by injury and the loss to the touring team was considerable. John had developed in the mould of W. H. T. Davies, for he was particularly deceptive with his casual approach, and Edwards was much harder and more experienced and the two were indeed, like 'bacon and eggs'. Off the field they were great friends with a healthy respect for each other. John the gentle, lucid talker on the game, and Edwards the prime enthusiast, eager and willing, enjoying the game's challenge.

Last year, the world of rugby recognised them as the top pair, for John took over from Gibson and Watkins while Edwards assumed the mantle of Catchpole, although South Africans would readily dispute the Welsh claim and offer the likeable and experienced Dawie de Villiers as the World's No. 1. In 1970, both were bedevilled by injuries and were not at their best. They played only six times together for Cardiff and in four matches for Wales. Both played poorly against Ireland in Dublin but Edwards returned to form before the end of season. Both players should challenge in 1971.

Edwards has power, and a pass as long and as accurate as

anything seen in recent years, although he was not a good passer of the ball at first. He is a strong, deceptive runner and an excellent place and drop-kicker, while his punting is accurate. He can survive hard knocks and after being buried on the cricket pitch at Loftus Versveld, beneath the whole Springbok pack, he has qualified for the title of the 'pocket Hercules', at least in British rugby. The Rugby League continue to offer him large sums to turn professional and it remains to be seen as to how long he can refuse them.

John works for a finance company and likes driving fast cars. He has the coolness of a racing car ace, and is a perfectly balanced runner with a ghost-like movement that enables him to weave through defences as did W. T. H. Davies in the days before the War and afterwards with the Rugby League. His try against England in April 1969 was as good as any scored by his predecessors, while he punts beautifully and drops for goal with accuracy. He covers well, too, and can stand up to hard forward play as he proved in New Zealand. John, like Edwards, is a quality player and together they are a formidable pair, yes, as necessary to Welsh rugby's success as are bacon and eggs for the game's supporters!

R. B. Hiller

When the International Board, in March 1969, amended the laws or, at least, rewrote them so that they were easier to understand, they paid one player, in particular, the compliment of adjusting the law to help him and players like him. They included in Law Five, dealing with 'Time', allowance for any time lost during the taking of a kick at goal, so as not to over-penalise the opposition. Certain place-kickers take great care of the placing of the ball and the lining up of the kick, and this tends to irritate the supporters of the other side. It has often led to booing and cat-calling and players have come under fire from crowds.

In an era when place-kicking is vital and, sad to say, a more frequent method of winning matches than by the scoring of tries, it is only just since the law allows it that a place-kicker, who takes a deep interest in the art of kicking, should be allowed time to do so, and given a fair crack of the whip by crowds. This is what the International Board intend, and as long as there is no 'indirect' penalty award and so many infringements carry a kick at goal punishment, then if the law allows it and the referee awards it, the kicker should be given his chance in fair conditions.

One successful kicker who has suffered in recent years from the cat-calling of the crowds is England's full-back Robert Hiller. Not that it has affected him unduly for he has put them over, in silence and in bedlam, and his country owes him much for his efforts. He has proved their top scorer and match saver, and with the British Lions in South Africa in 1968 he revealed prolific form as a kicker.

On July 17 at East London he scored 23 of his side's 26 points against Border to record the largest individual total by a Lion in South Africa with five penalties, two dropped goals, a conversion and a try. It was a fine effort and only two points short of the equally splendid effort by Malcolm Thomas for the Lions during the 1959 tour in New Zealand. In all Hiller scored 108 points in eight appearances on tour in 1968.

This total included 19 conversions, 18 penalty goals, two dropped goals and two tries, which indicates the accuracy of Hiller as a kicker with the big match temperament. He prepares his 'mound' carefully for the teeing of the ball and then takes some time 'laying the ball'. When this is done he stands, with feet together, before taking a certain number of paces backwards as required for the kick. Then he stands feet together again; takes a big breath to clear his lungs, fixes his eye on the ball, and then moves off after what appears to be an agonising wait for the opposition. With long strides he arrives at the point of impact with his left foot accurately placed, adjacent to the ball, and his right foot hitting hard and straight through while following through with head well down.

Cool as the proverbial cucumber, Hiller is a restless player; one could almost call him a 'happy wanderer' at full-back, and not everyone's ideal of what a player in the position should be like, but he is often exciting to watch. Hiller can be caught out of position, as he has been in important matches; he is mainly a one-footed kicker and not an outstanding punter with his left foot in the manner of greater players in the position.

It is said of him that he lacks speed, but he is a good runner with the ball; a more than useful sevens player, who enjoys opening up from the full-back position and entering 'the line'. I am sure that he could play at centre and outside half in club football without any difficulty. He can swerve and side-step, and used to enjoy very much the freedom of practice matches on tour, when he was known as the 'Boss man', and amused his opponents by chatting gaily as he played and issuing challenges. Hiller in his rugby is a Barbarian at heart, and one tends to think when watching him in action that he is not giving his whole attention to the task in hand. This is quite a false impression for Hiller is trying hard and in times of stress, as for England against Wales at Cardiff in April 1969, he is everywhere. In that match, he appeared to be playing Wales on his own at times and gave an outstanding exhibition of defensive play and place-kicking against the wind when his forwards were being overrun. He proved himself that day.

Robert Hiller is a Londoner and his 'cockney accent' at party-time is quite amusing. He was educated at Bec School before entering Birmingham University to gain a B.Sc. degree and then did a post-graduate course for a Dip. Ed. at St. Edmund's Hall, Oxford. He is a good games player and while at Oxford achieved a double 'blue' at rugby and cricket during his year, 1965-66. His rugby appearance in December 1965 was in a drawn match while his cricket appearance helped produce a big win by an innings over Cambridge. He opened the attack for Oxford and took three wickets for 48 runs in the second innings.

He played for the Harlequins after Oxford and soon revealed his ability as a match-winner with his enterprising play at full-back and his place-kicking. Hiller returned to his old school as a master and helped with games before winning his first cap for England against Wales at Twickenham. Rutherford had played against the New Zealanders in the November before the selectors decided to give the confident Hiller his chance, for in the previous season he had performed special feats for Surrey in the county championship, winning matches and saving them with last-minute goals, kicked from the touch-lines

He was a crowd-puller, and in his first match for England his side rather let Wales 'off the hook', but although he made one mistake which led to a try he played extremely well and, as he said, 'That knock-on in front of my own posts was really nasty. The ball seemed to check in its flight and dropped short.' Fortunately, the England selectors did not penalise him for this one error and his last-minute penalty goal against Ireland at Twickenham saved the match. Hiller got two more penalty goals against France in Paris and then a penalty and a conversion at Murrayfield. A tally of 22 points in his first four matches for England was a good start to his representative career, and this was followed by 104 points for the Lions, and then another good season in 1969 with 36 points for England. He captained England in 1970 and led his country to victory over South Africa and Ireland but was dropped for the French match rather unkindly.

Hiller is now 28 years of age and should certainly win more caps, for he is a big strong fellow, weighing nearly 14 st. and standing 6 ft. 2 in. His casual approach belies a shrewdness that serves him well and Hiller enjoys his rugby football, although at times he may appear surly on the field of play, especially when he executes a fierce hand-off. Off the field he is a cheerful, confident character with a dry sense of wit and the ability to laugh. This is good, for rugby has become a rather serious affair in recent years.

T. J. Kiernan

In rugby football it takes an Irishman to disarm the critics
and this, perhaps, could be one of the reasons why so many
Irishmen have led Lions' teams abroad. It is a long and
imposing list, starting with Dr. Tom Smyth in 1910 and
following with Sammy Walker in 1938, Dr. Karl Mullen
in 1950, Robin Thompson in 1955, Ronnie Dawson in 1959
and Tom Kiernan in 1968. There have been six Scottish
captains and seven Englishmen, but no Welshman. The
Irishmen, in general, have made a good job of it and although
only Thompson was able to share a Test series, many of these
captains led effective and popular sides.

Kiernan, a Cork accountant, led the last Lions' side in
South Africa, and though his team did not win a Test, he
was the outstanding figure in the series. Playing in all four
Tests, he scored all but three of the points achieved by his
side's tally of 38 points with 11 penalty goals and a conversion. On previous tours such accuracy would have proved
match winning, but in 1968 the Lions could score only one
try in four Tests, which was a feature quite out of character
with previous tours. Kiernan's effort shone like a beacon
across an arid desert and created a new record for an
individual player in a Test series in South Africa.

The most capped full-back in world rugby, he had made
42 appearances for Ireland before the 1970 International
season after being first capped against England in 1960 at the
age of 21. It is quite a remarkable record of consistency and
he has fought off many a worthy challenge from rival players
for the position during the last 10 seasons of top-class rugby
and he became a fixture in the Irish side because of his
ability to produce his best on the big occasion. Like all great
artists in sport, he is at his best when the pressure is on and
never ready to admit defeat.

Kiernan has a delightful personality in the best mould of

Irishmen. He is shrewd, evocative yet understanding;
extremely intelligent and sensitive beneath his carefree
exterior. His wit is quick and manner charming, but he is
sharp to defend his beliefs and his fellows, while the cause of
rugby union football and that of his beloved Ireland are very
near and dear to his big heart. It is difficult not to like and
admire Kiernan, even though at times one may disagree with
him. A devoted family man, he enjoys company; is a good
mixer and ready to discuss the game rationally at any time,
but often severe in his criticism of those who do not try to
understand the problems of the modern game.

Having known Kiernan throughout his career, I have seen
him mature and wear the mantle of responsibility easily, for
it has never caused his shoulders to stoop! The smile of the
'little people', infectious and amusing, has remained with
him and although in the stern moments of a Test match he
may look grave and concerned, he is there ready to cajole and
encourage his team. Yet he can be deeply hurt, as he
was when a journalist wrote a piece about the Lions as 'hotel
breakers'. The criticism merely served to increase his
loyalty, but the sadness of it all was that some of the mud
thrown in ignorance stuck. Kiernan is a diplomat as all
who heard his speech at the Springs Town Hall before Prime
Minister Vorster, after O'Shea had been sent off, will agree.
He did not deny the correctness of the referee's decision,
because Kiernan is an honest man in rugby football. He loves
a practical joke and good fun and was as ready to entertain
as any tourist.

He has been concerned always at the lack of success of
British Lions teams during the 1960's and the fact that since
1951 Irish sides have got near to, but never achieved, the
Championship or Triple Crown. He says: 'The lack of
success in the 1960's of the Lions has led to a depressed
attitude in these Islands, although I feel sure that coaching,
especially in the schools, will improve the situation. I would
feel it beneficial if the Lions were to play in Great Britain and
Ireland, for then their team-work would match the Southern

Hemisphere countries. Again the dispensation touch-kicking law should prove a stimulus which should be of benefit to those who are prepared to challenge rather than take the refuge of the touch area.' One cannot but agree that a Lions' side in action at home against touring teams would be an excellent idea and ensure greater continuity in the approach and composition of our sides, while the dispensation law has already brightened the game at club and international level in these Islands.

Thomas Joseph Kiernan was born at Cork in January, 1939, and is one of a family of five children with one brother and three sisters. He attended Presentation College, Cork, and then the local university and later qualified as a chartered accountant. His introduction to rugby football occurred at the age of five years—he could not have been younger—and his aptitude for the game was developed at school. He played for the university with distinction from 1957 to 1963 and was capped from there, much to the delight of local enthusiasts and Noel Murphy, his cousin, who was already in the national side.

He toured with the Lions in 1962 and played in one Test as John Willcox, of England, was the first choice at full-back, although Kiernan had been with the Irish side to South Africa in 1961. When Ireland made a second tour, to Australia in 1967, he was the captain and made a good job of it, an achievement which earned him the captaincy of the 1968 Lions, again in South Africa.

Kiernan regards the honour as the greatest of his career, while the Irish Test win in Australia in 1967 was the one that gave him greatest satisfaction. Perhaps, if he continues to play, having passed J. W. Kyle's record of 46 appearances, he will regard his 47th appearance for Ireland as the most important moment of his career. Whether he does matters not, for Kiernan has written his name boldly in the record books as a full-back, sound at catching and kicking and exceptionally good at place-kicking when the occasion demanded it.

A. E. I. Pask

Alun Edward Islwyn Pask was an unusual player, but never-theless an outstanding one, who made 26 consecutive appear-ances for Wales as a forward, plus one in an unofficial inter-national match against Fiji, which is the longest run without being dropped by a forward in the history of Welsh rugby. He was selected for one more match, but had to withdraw owing to the death of his brother David, who was also a fine player and leader.

He was 29 years of age when playing his last match for Wales and retired at the end of that season in April 1967. Prior to winning his first cap against France in Paris in 1961, he had been a reserve for his country on no fewer than 13 occasions. Throughout his career he remained loyal to his club, Abertillery, and although it was often said of him that he was not always at his best for his club, he was one of those players who needed the big occasion to bring out the best in him. Selectors, both national and international, were often divided in their opinion as to what was his best position in the pack. However, he was first and foremost a No. 8 forward, although frequently appearing for the Lions and Wales on the flank.

Ideally built for the back-row of the scrum, he stood 6 ft. 3 in. and weighed over 15 st. His long legs carried him quickly over the ground and his safe hands and basketball experience made him one of the best handlers of the ball in British rugby at forward. His knowledge of the game was considerable and although he did his work in the tight and often especially well in the mud, as against England at Cardiff in 1965 and against Scotland at Cardiff in 1966, he was a brilliant open field player. His covering was amazingly accurate and long will I remember his chasing tackle of

161

French wing Rancoule, at Cardiff in 1962, which saved the match for Wales and proved his worthiness to tour as a Lion that year in South Africa.

In attack, he thoroughly enjoyed himself and his ability to carry the ball one-handed and use it to deceive opponents as they attempted to tackle him was never better illustrated than in the memorable and exciting match against Fiji in 1964. This was the rugby at which Pask excelled and it is little wonder that he is regarded in South Africa, where the going is generally firm, as one of the great loose forwards of his era.

As a leader of Wales he was not as successful as Gwilliam, mainly because he expected all men to give of their best when playing for their country rather than their having to be exhorted to the utmost. Had he possessed the schoolmaster approach of Gwilliam, or the supreme confidence of Rowlands, he would have enjoyed even greater success. However, he led Wales to the Championship title in 1966 and was desperately unlucky not to be nominated by the four Home Unions as leader for the Lions' tour of that year. However much sympathy one has, and there must be a great deal for Campbell-Lamerton, the four Home Unions' tours committee did a considerable injustice to Pask in not appointing him the touring captain.

Pask never complained and was extremely loyal to Campbell-Lamerton throughout the tour, but I believe the 'unfriendly rebuff' made a deep impression on the player, since he was never quite the same on his return, having lost some of that quiet determination he showed on the big occasion. At all times he attempted to enjoy his rugby, believing it to be a game that was intended for enjoyment, and Pask managed to hide his disappointment effectively and he was much liked by his fellows, although occasionally suffering severely at the hands of critics, official and unofficial, and sometimes administrators who appeared to prefer more vigorous methods rather than the delicate skills and touches of genius that Pask so frequently provided.

At the end of the line-out Pask was particularly successful, either palming down or taking the ball cleanly to work in close co-operation with his scrum-half. It was during his career in the game that the back-row approach in the British Isles was subjected to change and closer co-operation with the scrum-half in attack was developed to make his the key position behind the scrum.

Pask began his rugby career at the age of twelve at Pontllanfraith Grammar School, where he was a successful scrum-half at first, which enabled him to learn the basic skills of the game. By the time he entered the sixth form he was in the pack and awarded a Welsh Secondary Schools' cap on three occasions before entering the Army to do his National Service. At 19 he was in the Parachute Regiment, where he met and formed a lifelong friendship with Haydn Morgan. They both returned to Abertillery in December 1956 and joined the local club, where cheerful chairman Ron Jones encouraged them to become permanent members of the side. However, on being demobbed, Pask entered Loughborough College.

This enabled him to develop both his physical and rugby skills and he played with distinction for his college, Leicestershire and the UAU. In the 1958-59 season he captained Loughborough and appeared in his first Welsh trial. It was the first of 13 trials and there followed 13 nominations as a Welsh reserve. As Pask says, 'Before I finally received my first cap, against France in Paris in March 1961, I thought I would never play for Wales!' Davidge had to withdraw from the Welsh side and Pask won his first cap as a flank forward. In the following season Nash was originally selected at No. 8 against England but withdrew on the morning of the match and Pask played and remained a constant member of the Welsh side until his retirement.

On Lions tours he was unlucky with injuries, suffering a damaged rib in the Third Test in South Africa in 1962 and a broken collarbone in the Fourth Test in New Zealand in 1966. I shall never forget the sight of the Welsh Lions crowding into his hotel room at Auckland following the second injury, keeping him company with cheerful banter instead of whooping it up and leaving him alone. Surely, this was a true indication of the high esteem in which he was held by his fellow Welsh players. Pask was an outstanding player; a perfectionist, and established himself as a player of world class, especially as a No. 8 forward.

M. C. R. Richards

New Zealanders are not readily given to praise of players from other countries and thus the general agreement at the end of the 1969 Welsh tour in New Zealand that Maurice Charles Rees Richards was 'the greatest' wing in contemporary rugby is something the modest young Welshman can accept with pride. From March 1968 to June 1969 he crowded more success into 16 months than most players enjoy in a whole career in the game. In this time he made nine appearances for Wales and played three tests for the British Lions while visiting South Africa, Rhodesia, New Zealand, Australia, Fiji and France. For any rugby player this is quite an achievement, but for one born and bred in the historic Rhondda Valley, it is an achievement to be treasured.

Yet Richards was a capable wing for many years before the Welsh selectors saw fit to honour him, and thus it was almost inevitable that Richards would succeed and not become a one-cap wonder. He took to representative rugby quickly and calmly, like a player who had been specially groomed for the task. More important, he became a better player, and went on improving until in New Zealand in 1969 he earned the title of 'the greatest' of the moment in the world game.

Richards is a try-getter and what better asset could be possessed by a player appearing on the wing? He has scored tries where few other players would have done so, and this is not an extravagant claim, even though there have been many remarkable players in the position down through the years. Various wings have had various attributes, but few have possessed the many skills of the modest Richards.

When he scored four tries for Wales against England at Cardiff in April 1969, he equalled the Welsh record, held for 70 years by the illustrious Willie Llewellyn, the oldest surviving Welsh international, who watched the Richards' performance on TV. Later the two players met at a reception and as they are both Rhondda born, it was delightful to admire their modesty and warm affection for each other's ability. Llewellyn was pleased that Richards had equalled the record and Richards proud to have done so, for like all young Welshmen he had learned much about the greatness of Llewellyn. However, even now, he does not see himself as another Llewellyn, despite his achievements, for only time and the homage to his record by successive generations can gain him a place in the Welsh hall of fame. That is the way of Wales, and especially of rugby football!

After seeing him wasted virtually as a match-winner with the Lions in South Africa in 1968 through lack of opportunity, I wondered whether he would ever receive the ball to run, as did the legendary Webb Ellis in 1823, and produce a renaissance in wing threequarter play. Richards has always fascinated me as a runner, but his 'starvation' diet of passes in South Africa disappointed and I felt that a wing was becoming nothing more than a thrower-in of the ball at a line-out and the collector of kicks ahead in defence. It was so sad; so depressing, and a damaging feature of the game as a spectacle.

Then suddenly Wales, in contrast to other countries, employed the national squad system in 1968-69 and returned to basic principles. 'Win the ball quickly and get it to the wings,' was the maxim, and as a result Richards scored six tries in the four international matches and everyone was delighted with the resurgence of wing play. In New Zealand he played in six matches and collected six tries, which produced twelve tries for him in 12 matches in the scarlet jersey of his country.

Richards returned home from New Zealand a king among wings, and a match-winner, even though he could not gain enough ball to do so in the two Tests against New Zealand, and at 24 years of age was the world's No. 1 player in his position. Born at Ystrad Rhondda in February 1945, he is the grandson of Edwin Rees, a former professional with Charlton Athletic and Bradford City.

Educated at Tonypandy Grammar School, where he was first introduced to the game, and from where he played for the Welsh Secondary Schools in 1961-62 and 1962-3, Richards developed an ambition after playing at the Arms Park for the Schools to play for the Cardiff Club. He appeared for them in the 1963-64 season, including the match against the All-Blacks, and then achieved a final Welsh trial. In the next season he appeared in the Welsh XV against Fiji but had to wait until 1968, despite several additional trials, to win his first cap against Ireland and, as he says, 'Running out on to the field in the scarlet jersey of Wales for the first time will remain my proudest moment!'

From that moment he never looked back and remains a model for young players to follow since he does not smoke, is a teetotaller and deeply interested in his chapel. He keeps himself remarkably fit and takes each match seriously. Richards is try-hungry, for after scoring four for Wales he commented, 'I wish I had scored six!'

He is a keen student of the game, although especially interested in athletics and badminton and feels that there is too much emphasis placed on goal-kicking. 'It plays too vital a part,' he says, 'as not all the offences in matches should result in penalty kicks at goal. Too much rests on the "judgment" of referees, as the laws are too complicated.' Richards goes on to say, 'With so many midweek matches in Wales, not enough time is devoted to team training, coaching and fitness. Again, climatic conditions for two months of the season make things so difficult that there is a genuine case for a mid-season break.

'Few sides appear prepared to adopt a handling approach with the emphasis on the movement of the ball when the situation permits, rather than position on the field of play and the nature of the score at that moment. Finally, loose-rucking in the British Isles is just not good enough!' Richards is so right, and his comments indicate what players think is required to improve the game. As Richards has proved—it pays to keep the wings running! Sad that he should turn professional before the start of the 1969-70 season.

P. G. D. Robbins

Certain rugby players are unlucky in various ways, but few in recent times have been as unlucky as Peter Robbins, who was denied an overseas tour because of successive injuries after being selected. Undoubtedly, one of the outstanding English back-row forwards of the post-War years, he deserved a Lions' tour and would have been an invaluable member of the 1959 team in Australia and New Zealand, but he broke a leg on Easter Tuesday before the tour while playing for the Barbarians against Newport. He regarded his invitation to tour with the Lions as one of the two proudest moments in his rugby career and the disappointment of not being able to travel remained with him for many years. However, now he has retired, he treats the matter lightly, but there were few keener players than he and few more astute observers following the game at the moment.

Robbins played through an era when the tactical approach of flank forward play changed considerably. Yet he possessed the knowledge, strength and enthusiasm to adapt himself to changing conditions and earned for himself the reputation of being a most difficult player, tactically, to play against. Perhaps his greatest single duel on the rugby field was for England against Wales in 1958, when he spent the afternoon at Twickenham trying to curtail the activities of Cliff Morgan.

They were worthy antagonists, as each had studied the other's approach in detail, and Morgan attempted to hug the one touch-line away from the swirling wind to nullify a slight advantage held by the England forwards while Robbins, in turn, attempted to contain Morgan by driving him backwards and towards the touch-line, so as to narrow the angle of Morgan's touch kick. It was an absorbing battle of wits and skills!

Peter George Derek Robbins was born in September 1933 and educated at Bishop Vesey's Grammar School, Sutton Coldfield, but first played the game at 11 years of age at King Henry VIII School, Coventry. Easily adapting himself to the requirements of rugby football, he won a schoolboy cap in both grades before entering St. Edmund Hall, Oxford, and winning four blues in 1954-55-56-57. He was on the winning and losing sides twice apiece during this period but admits he was never happier than when leaving the field in December 1957, after Oxford had achieved a narrow victory by a try to nil. He had played an important part in the victory by his leadership as captain and his spoiling of the equally experienced J. P. Horrocks-Taylor at outside-half for Cambridge.

Robbins, like those before him, was proud to have led an Oxford side to victory and there are few who have appeared in four successive Varsity matches, while in the same season he played in the centre for his College with J. R. C. Young, and won the Cuppers Final for the third successive year! At the time, Robbins was at the height of his career as a backrow forward, having been capped for the first time for England against Wales at Twickenham in 1956, and went on to make 19 appearances for his country. He was an invaluable member of the 1957 and 1958 sides which, under the captaincy of Eric Evans, won the Championship, and in 1957 achieved the 'Grand Slam' as well as the defeat of a touring team, for the first time since 1928.

During this time Robbins was an automatic choice for England, the Barbarians and touring teams, and should have gone to South Africa in May 1958 with the Barbarians, but, after being selected on the Sunday during the Easter tour in South Wales, injured himself in the swimming baths at Penarth and this prevented him from travelling. When he suffered a second injury, also with the Baa-Baas in the following year and could not go to New Zealand with the Lions, his cup of woe was full to overflowing, but he soldiered on bravely and although making his last appearance for England against Scotland in 1962 in a drawn game at Murrayfield, he was not chosen to tour with the 1962 Lions in South Africa. Few post-War players have been more deserving of a Lions tour than Robbins and he must be considered as one of England's unluckiest players.

Robbins, though a lively personality with a ready wit and sharp comment, is dedicated to the game and one of the most knowledgeable authorities on back-row play. It requires hard work to become a good flank forward and, as he says, 'The back row is often over-glamorised, but to a certain extent it is often the most exciting position to play in. There is a lot of scope in attack and defence but the job needs concentration with power and patience.'

Many a time I have sat up with Robbins, Bleddyn Williams and rugby officials chatting, instead of sleeping on the night sleeper from Edinburgh to Birmingham, following an international match at Murrayfield. Never afraid to put his own viewpoint, clearly and technically, Robbins has much to offer in the way of ideas and advice while keeping pace with the changing needs of the game. Never was he more depressed than at the end of the Wales v England match in Cardiff in 1969 and he could only utter the comment, 'We must do something about our (English) forward play!'

Standing six feet and weighing 14½ stones Robbins was the ideal build for a flank forward. He was strong in the hips and shoulders and blessed with good hands, which enabled him to work extremely well at the line-out and in the loose, push his weight in the set scrums, dribble accurately and tackle like a demon. The leading outside-halves of his era rate him very highly in the list of most-difficult opponents to play against. His views on the modern game are interesting and, as rugby correspondent of the *Financial Times*, he is afforded the opportunity of studying the game closely, particularly at international level. However, until recently he was engaged in schoolmastering and this enabled him to undertake coaching, which is very close to his heart.

He told me recently, 'There is a great need for some sort of knock-out competition on the French system, but not involving relegation and promotion. Again, I feel that the field is far too crowded at the moment, and the game would be more fluid if there were only 13 players a side. This is justified by the success of sevens rugby. Spectators do enjoy spectacular play, but this is so rare because of a wrong and mistaken mental approach on the part of the players, and an over-populated playing area.' Robbins went on to say, 'I would dearly love to see the differential penalty, and the Price-Murphy affair at Cardiff in 1969 should have seen the award of a penalty to Ireland under the Welsh posts. This would curb the miscreants, but the referees will have to be strong men of integrity, and players must learn that the referee is in sole charge!'

Robbins himself was a hard, but controlled player, and had a great rival during his career in R. C. C. Thomas, of Wales. Their approach to the game was quite similar and they achieved much by thinking about each match beforehand. Each player had stamina in excess and this served them well at all times. I recall, recently, sitting up all night on a cross-channel steamer, from Dover to Calais, chatting about rugby football with Robbins and other friends and not having a wink of sleep before reaching Paris at 8 a.m. As we said cheerio, until the next day, at the Garde du Nore, Robbins said casually, 'Now I'm going to play for the British Veterans against the French Veterans!' It was discovered later that Robbins had played at scrum-half and done extremely well. No wonder he was a success at top level!

D. P. Rogers, O.B.E.

It is always an achievement to become the record cap-holder in one's country, and especially when the previous record has stood for over 30 years. For Derek Prior Rogers it was a special achievement since he passed the record of an illustrious player and England captain, W. W. Wakefield, now Lord Wakefield of Kendall. Rogers achieved his record while leading England in 1969 and one of the first to congratulate him was the noble lord. Later the Queen honoured him with the O.B.E.

Rogers was first capped in 1961 against Ireland and his play has been consistent, to say the least, for he missed only seven matches in nine seasons after being first capped, and although he did not play against South Africa during this period for England, he appeared in two Tests for the British Lions in the 1962 South African tour. Thus he has played against all countries and toured abroad with the Barbarians, whom he has captained, and enjoyed a full career in the game as a lively hard-working, determined flank forward. Rogers never tires of rugby beacuse he really enjoys playing in any grade.

Rogers was born at Bromham in Bedfordshire in June 1939 and is one of two sons. He was educated at Bedford School and City University and the mere fact that he went to Bedford School would have given delight to the late E. D. H. Sewell, but his record-breaking appearances would have had that notable critic dancing on the tiles at Twickenham. His introduction to rugby football occurred on his entering Bedford School in 1950 where he made the School XV in 1955 and two years later he appeared for the famous Bedford Club while still at school, serving the club loyally ever since.

At 18 years of age he had his first taste of senior football and played in the 1957-58 season for the East Midlands. Then came England trials and while he argues that his fair hair helped him catch the eyes of the selectors, it was his play for a brave Midland Counties XV against the 1960 Springboks that really decided his future in the game. As a 21-year-old, with the formidable Don White on the other flank of the scrum, he impressed the tourists, but just failed to make the England XV against them.

Rogers became a Barbarian in 1961 and then a Lion in 1962, followed by tours to New Zealand with England in 1963 and to Canada in 1966, and then with the Barbarians to South Africa in 1969. For him it has been a busy career, but he regards his two proudest moments as his first cap and the first time he led England. 'It is a great thrill to don the white jersey for the first time and an even greater one to lead England on to the field,' he admits modestly, for Rogers is nothing if not modest.

His outstanding asset is his industry on the field of play, for he is tireless and thoroughly enjoys the freedom of his position as flank-forward and the variety in it. Taking the place of such an outstanding player as Peter Robbins was a difficult task, but Rogers was encouraged, and although a completely different player in approach, held his place against all rivals for a long time. His own motto is 'Death to the fly-half', and he has a singleness of purpose in his play, for he believes that one must chase the ball continuously, but never allow the opposing outside-half out of one's sight!

Rogers is conscientious and this is proved by the fact that he admits to being nervous before every international match. He is a happy but quiet tourist for he is not a 'wrecker' or 'burner', but always friendly and loyal. He does not smoke and drinks very little, but has a sense of fun and eats well. On tour he enjoys his food but, fortunately, he never puts on weight and, throughout his career, his 'just under 14 stones' has never varied. His fitness has never been in doubt at any time, although he has suffered several nasty injuries.

Many at odd times have attempted practical jokes
against him, but he has taken it all in his stride and on the
occasion of his birthday, June 30, 1962, at Port Elizabeth, he
was presented with a hairnet and a set of hairpins! It was an
attempt to force him to get a hair-cut because his fair hair
stood out from his skull-cap. He likes fast cars and drives well
himself, particularly on the M 1. Rogers is not a 'late night
man' or an extrovert in the game, preferring to lead by
example at the head of his pack in attack and alongside his
backs in defence. Never is he afraid to fall in defence, while
he does not suffer fools gladly, as one New Zealand player
will confirm!

Rogers plays hard but cleanly and doesn't take kindly to
obstruction and nonsense. Complicated manoeuvres do not
impress him greatly, neither do constant changes in the laws,
for as he says, 'The modern game is in a healthy state and
I view leagues and K.O. competitions with considerable
reservation. I agree, of course, that playing standards must
be improved, but to do so we need more players who are
prepared to put themselves out at club level.'

Rogers is a traditionalist; a true club man and, as such is
an excellent example to young people in the game. He is
essentially English in belief, approach and execution. He is
an 80-minute man and feels that rugby is a game that requires
all-out effort and not too much 'chat'. Nowadays, there is a
great deal of theory and discussion, but Rogers believes in
getting on with it!

He is now a marketing consultant, but qualified as an
electrical engineer with a diploma in technology. He plays
golf and tennis quite well and is particularly keen on the cult
of physical fitness, but not in a New Zealand sense, for he has
many interests outside sport and one of these is the study
and collection of antiques.

As a sportsman he is a pleasant, energetic fellow and one
whose head will never be disturbed by the fact that he
possesses an outstanding record. In the England side against
Wales at Cardiff in 1969, which was his 34th appearance,

the next most capped player was Finlan with 11. So Rogers will hold the record for many seasons to come and deserves the accolade of the Order of the British Empire.

D. C. T. Rowlands

This is the story of a player who is in the process of changing into an 'alickadoo', and he is a personality and character whom you either admire or violently disagree with in the game. In actual fact he is a cheerful chap; a good Welshman, and relationships with him improve on maturity. At first many thought he was something of a rugby showman, but time has proved him to be keen, hard-working and loyal to the game. That is all one can ask of an 'alickadoo'. As a player he proved himself by leading Wales on 14 consecutive occasions from the scrum-half position and sharing one championship in 1964 before winning the Championship and Triple Crown in 1965. He was something of a contro-versial player, not loved by everyone, but he never hid his intentions and got his men to follow him through rough times and smooth and, following a couple of seasons helping Swansea after leaving the national XV, he retired and sud-denly flashed into the rugby administrative headlines with a series of appointments that almost took his breath away. He became the national team coach in a plan to sweep away the cobwebs of tradition and lead Wales into the exclusive, modern world of power rugby.

The man is Daniel Clive Thomas Rowlands, now a sales representative and formerly student and physical education master who has always been rugby mad. He has always sur-prised rugby men by popping up when least expected and succeeding. Outspoken, fiercely partisan and confident, he will have always an equal number of admirers and critics but such a state of affairs causes him little concern. Rowlands is an extrovert, but a pleasant one, and proud of it, and while he can coerce a side to play really hard there is no malice in him. He is a fiery Welshman, not always happy with the protocol of rugby, a bit of a rebel, but essentially a man of West Wales, the place of his birth and upbringing.

Rowlands was born in 1939 when the lights in Europe went out before the terror of Hitler, and when rugby football was placed in cold storage until 1945. By then the young toddler had started school where he lived at Cwmtwrch, a word difficult to pronounce for all except Welshmen. From this village he graduated to Ystradgynlais Grammar School, where his sportsmaster, Peter Woodman, directed him along the road to fame and his first adventure was with the Welsh Secondary Schools 'Dragons' who visited South Africa in 1956. He was a wing-forward turned scrum-half, and I recall him listening with the team when I lectured them about South Africa at the R.A.F. Station, St. Athan, before they left on tour. It was a successful trip under Ned Gribble and Rowley Jones, and Rowlands gained a thirst for big rugby.

He did two years national service as a radar mechanic in the R.A.F. before entering the Cardiff College of Education and played on vacation for Abercrave in the West Wales Rugby Union. This was a hard apprenticeship and produced a resilience in Rowands that stood him in good stead for the hard days ahead in senior rugby. At College, Roy Bish, now coach to the Cardiff Club, taught Rowlands the theory and mechanics of the game and he became a power at scrum-half in a successful College 1st XV. With him were many other young players destined to shine in the senior clubs of Wales. In his last two years he led the College side and it was this experience that prepared him for national leadership, and since those days he has always enjoyed directing operations. He liked having his 'own way' in the game because he felt his way was the right way. Many argued that his approach was too confined but he got his team all working together and enforced discipline as few Welsh leaders had done before him. Only John Gwilliam had a superior touch, for while Rowlands always reminded me of the teacher in charge, some said a conductor, Gwilliam was the headmaster. Both effective; both successful, and both criticised all too readily, but both have their names in the record books of success. They have been Triple Crown leaders.

His initial first-class club was Llanelli, but after taking an appointment as a P.E. teacher in Cwmbran he joined Ponty-pool, and it was from this club that he stepped into the Welsh XV in 1963 as a captain of an untried side on his first appear-ance. Many criticised the selection; I did myself, feeling it was too great a gamble and unfair to the young player. His first season was not a successful one for Wales, but in 1963-64 the Welsh XV began to take shape and the championship was shared with Scotland, before there followed another set-back, the South African tour of 1964, and then eventual success and the fulfilment of an ambition for Rowlands.

In 1965 he led a fine Welsh side, full of outstanding players, to a Triple Crown victory beating England, Scotland and Ireland before losing to an inspired French XV in Paris. This was the 14th and last appearance by Rowlands for his country and his only regret as a player was his misfortune not to make a Lions' tour and be honoured as a Barbarian. Yet he has visited South Africa, New Zealand, Australia and Fiji to further his rugby education.

He moved back to the West after leaving teaching for business as a sales representative, first with an oil company and now with a tobacco company, and joined the Swansea Club, to whom he gave two years of loyal service, the second as captain of the club. He retired at 29 and bid for a place as a vice-president on the Welsh Rugby Union, gaining the seat caused by the death of former president, Cliff Prosser. This was an achievement at the first time of asking, but better was to follow for him as a 'rumpus' about coaching caused an 'about turn' on the part of the executive and he was a last-minute appointment as honorary coach to the Welsh touring party in the Argentine in September 1968. Yet, in keeping the pattern of his career, his first outing as an official and coach was not blessed with success on the field. Rowlands

Left: Tom Kiernan. *Right:* Cliff Davies, on extreme right, waits
to be presented to President Auriol before the France v Wales
match, 1947.

Gareth Edwards.

D. P. Rogers, Captain of England, in action against Wales at Cardiff, April 1969.

Alun Pask scores a try for Wales against England at Twickenham in January 1966.

worked hard enough, but he had to learn as he went along.
He did learn and it came as no surprise, despite the challenge
of more-experienced coaches, that the WRU nominated him
as the honorary coach to the national XV for the 1968-69
season. Wales remained unbeaten and he was appointed
assistant manager for the tour in New Zealand but again
without success for Wales were beaten in the two vital tests.

His views on representative football are always interesting.
This is what he said after the Championship victory of 1965,
'The main tactics for any team, at any time, must be to win,
especially in International football. The end, I feel, justifies
the means. Without good forwards you have no chance of
success.' Talking about British rugby he said, 'The weather
dictates the British approach to the game, and for most of the
winter it is a fight against conditions. There is a certain
heavy ground tempo of play to which all players tend to
adjust themselves. Stamina, rather than outstanding speed,
is developed, and our national sides are more intent upon
reserves of stamina than bursts of speed.'

Rowlands told me this after his hour of triumph on the
field and four years later, following the defeats suffered by
Wales in New Zealand, he commented, 'It is back to square
one for us. The only way to equal the All Blacks perfection is
to start all over again at schoolboy level. It will take ten years.'
He was disappointed and gloomy but still prepared to fight
back. His spirit is not easily subdued and he is ready to spend
the next ten years preparing Welsh teams.

The question remains as to whether players during the
next ten years will dedicate themselves to the cause. Do
they want to approach the game in such a manner? It is
the new way of life that has changed so much and, consequently, it will become increasingly hard for British
coaches. However, Rowlands is as determined off the field as
he was on it. He means to get results, but will the challenge
prove too formidable?

J. W. Telfer

The great Scottish players are men of action rather than of words, and this may be a reason why rugby football in Scotland, has not blazed across that land, as in other countries. Scotland has fewer extroverts in the game than any of the International Board countries, and belives implicitly that the game is essentially for players. Press conferences, TV discussions, and outbursts in print are indeed rare, and I can think of not more than two Scottish players who have written anything in detail about the game, yet they all guard its ideals diligently.

They have been accused of conservatism, but if at the moment they appear old-fashioned in their beliefs, they are often prepared to die for them on the field of play. James William Telfer of Galashiels is such a Scot, although he is not old-fashioned. He is a man's man; a remarkably loyal and astute forward, and a leader of no mean standing. He is a true borderer, following in a line of splendidly determined borderers who have served their club, country and the British Lions' sides faithfully and successfully.

Telfer would have been a notable player in any era, because he is a technically sound player with strength and courage and a true understanding of what is required. I recall chatting briefly to him at the end of the test series between the Springboks and the Lions in 1968 for, as we passed each other in Ellis Park, he commented, 'We lost because we were not as efficient as our opponents in the basic skills.' He was absolutely right, for to Telfer the basic skills are all-important. His approach to rugby football is straightforward and simple, as he believes in nothing complicated and confusing. Telfer is an honest man, who speaks his mind to friend and foe, and never more sincerely than at Christchurch in 1966, after he had led the Lions in an unhappy match against Canterbury.

It had been a rough, dirty match and the Lions had received several uncalled for injuries, especially Macfadyean who was a clean player at all times. Telfer hit out hard at New Zealand rugby when he said, 'I am not going to say today's match was dirty, because every match in which I have played in New Zealand has been dirty!' These words struck home at the whole assembly beneath the grandstand at Lancaster Park, and they were given world-wide coverage by the Press and radio. To me, having watched much rugby in New Zealand, it had to be said, and said by a player; especially a man of few words, for it carried much greater criticism than if it had come from the pen of a critic or the mouth of a visiting administrator.

Telfer is a Scot, and many New Zealanders are of Scottish ancestry, and thus his words hit home. Some people agreed with him and argued that New Zealand should curtail their physical approach, bordering on intimidation. Administrators tried to 'whitewash' the whole thing—how silly they were— while some members of the Lions party said they did not agree with Telfer. This was diplomacy that failed the game in its hour of need. Telfer was right, and while I had always admired him previously, his courage and forthrightness on this special day warmed my heart.

There followed an even-rougher match at Auckland, when even New Zealand administrators had to call 'enough', but there still exists a painful arrogance about New Zealand rugby which could lose them many friends unless they use their remarkable ability in preference to their physical strength. Few players who have been there on tour have ever said they would prefer New Zealand rugby to their own. Telfer was one of those who criticised strongly while he was there, for he lacks nothing in courage and is always prepared to ruck hard and fall bravely to save. He suffered many injuries in 1966 and 1968 but always played on courageously. Rugby to him is still a game and, although he goes all out to win,

he believes in strict control of one's approach to the physical
side.

Telfer was born the only son of the family at Pathead,
Midlothian, in March, 1940, and was introduced to rugby at
Melrose Grammar School and developed his skill later at
Galashiels Academy. From there he went on to the Heriot
Watt College in Edinburgh, graduating in science, and
returned to teach at Galashiels Academy as well as taking a
special interest in coaching his pupils in rugby!

He joined the Melrose Club at the age of 17 years and has
played regularly in the 1st XV since that age, having had three
years in the School 1st XV to reveal himself as a player of
considerable promise. He was in the Border Schools XV that
played Wales in 1956, and in senior rugby he has appeared for
the South of Scotland in the provincial challenge since 1959.
In addition, Telfer has captained both his club and the
South of Scotland for four years and led the South of Scotland
side which toured South Africa in 1967.

He gained the first of his 21 caps in 1964; toured Canada
with his country in the same year, and travelled on three
Barbarian Easter tours in South Wales. His experiences with
the Lions in 1966 and 1968 developed his approach and he
has served his country well as a leader, regarding the honour
of leading Scotland against England at Murrayfield in 1968
as the greatest of his career. He has appeared in eight Test
matches for the Lions but, perhaps, played his greatest match
on tour, while leading the British against the Northern
Transvaal at Pretoria in July 1968.

He was escorted off, bleeding profusely, in the second half
with the Lions recovering bravely from a first half onslaught,
but still behind, and we thought he would not return, but
come back he did and shared in a tremendous victory. He
twisted his knee before the end but limped off, delighted,
and saying, 'This was the greatest victory in any match I have
played. It was wonderful to play in, and the lads were
superb.' Scots do not wear their hearts on their sleeves, but
this man had the courage of the famous 'Ladies from Hell',

and his opponents that day respected him, as they do in all countries.

Telfer is a good leader of forwards because he leads by example and, of those forwards I have watched in the British Isles during the 'sixties, I would always have him in my pack. With his sleeves rolled up, and his white scrum cap on his fair head, plus a bandage on his knee which is minus a cartilege, he can always be seen working, and in search of the ball. To him rugby is an affair of honour, and to do slightly less than one's best is a matter for self-reproach.

Off the field, like so many Scots before him, he is a quiet fellow although an ideal tourist as little disturbs him, and he is prepared to sit on the outside of the circle watching the extroverts perform while enjoying it all, very thoroughly. Some have criticised him on the field, saying he is not a number eight and a better blind side, but those who play with him respect and admire him.

He is now 30 years of age and coming to the end of a long career in the game, yet he will be remembered in many lands, as are leading Scottish forwards like McLeod, Rollo, Bannerman, Elliot, Kemp, Morrison, Bruce, Beattie, Robson and many others. Telfer is truly a Scottish forward of the best type and a man of action not words, but when he does speak he has something pertinent to say ... ask any New Zealander!

Stewart Wilson

To reach the top in the game and remain at the top, any player must enjoy good fortune as well as possessing the necessary ability and determination to succeed. This is true of most games but especially rugby football, and perhaps the unluckiest player of recent years, apart from those who have suffered serious injury like the amazing Danny Hearn and others, is the former Scottish full-back, Stewart Wilson. No player tried harder or was more loyal to the game than this pleasant young man who had ability and wanted to succeed. Unfortunately, the Goddess of Fortune played unkind tricks with him on the field of play and he was often robbed of the success he deserved.

Of all the place-kickers I have watched since the War, and they have been many in several lands, quite the unluckiest has been Stewart Wilson, and, like a golfer not striking the ball right, he tried everything possible. In New Zealand with the British Lions in 1966 he even accepted the kind offer of R. W. H. 'Bob' Scott to help, realising that Scott himself had suffered the same 'malaise' in South Africa in 1949. Just when Wilson was moving right and 'getting there' something would happen and he would miss vital goals by inches.

His technique was good and sound, but the ball, even when sailing for the target, would often veer just wide of the uprights before the end of its trajectory. My heart bled for Wilson on tour because he played so bravely and well as a full-back. If only he had enjoyed fifty per cent better fortune as a place-kicker, he would have been happy. In fact, he would have been hailed as one of the great ones to visit New Zealand, like Bassett of 1930, Jones of 1950 and Scotland and Davies of 1959, but Dame Fortune refused to smile on a young man who has always been extremely loyal to rugby football.

Wilson is now at the Stanford College business school in California for two years and at the age of 28 is out of British rugby for a while. He will play a few matches in the U.S.A. where rugby is growing apace, although, as he says, 'the demands of work at the school are very exacting', and he may not have much opportunity to do so. When he returns he will be 29 years of age and 'it may be too late to enjoy another year or so with a club', he argues, but if he follows in the footsteps of another clever young businessman who played for his country at full-back, K. J. F. Scotland, he will carry on for a few more years and enjoy himself.

Stewart Wilson was born the eldest of three sons, in the middle of World War II, at Downham Market, Norfolk. His

younger brother James, played for Oxford University in1967
and 1968 and his second brother, John, is at Leeds University.
A true Anglo-Scot, he was educated at Pinner County
Grammar School and then Oxford University where he
gained a 'blue' at full-back in 1963 and 1964. He first
appeared in a Scottish trial in 1962 at the age of 20 but was
not capped until the French match of 1964 after winning his
'blue'. During the 1964-65-66-67-68 seasons he made 22
appearances for Scotland, and only two Scottish full-backs,
Scotland and Drysdale, have made more than Wilson.

He toured the Argentine with the Combined Varsity side
in 1965 and then New Zealand, Australia and Canada with
the 1966 Lions. On the long and arduous tour 'down under'
he played in 20 matches and scored 89 points, and appeared
in six of the seven Tests against Australia, New Zealand and
Canada. On his return he played for Scotland in 1967 and
1968 and in his last season for Scotland and the Barbarians
against New Zealand, claiming in all, six Test appearances
against the All-Blacks, which enabled him to make an
extremely close and accurate study of the 'vigorous men from
down under', and he comments upon them as follows:

'Wales did us all proud in New Zealand with some
excellent results in the provincial matches but the All Backs
are a really great side at present and, of course, their own
ground and interpretations give them a start over visitors
which no one can afford against them. I think that perspective
will prove the All Blacks pack of the 1964-1970 era to be one
of the best, if not THE best, of all time. The 1966 Lions were
thought to be weak because of their lack of success against
them, but I feel now that we met them at their peak, although
we did not know it at the time. However, there is no need to
despair because Wales have proved that even a short two-year
period of organised coaching can bring demonstrable
improvements and, in the long run, more can be hoped for
if coaching is taken up on a wide scale in the other Home
Unions.'

Wilson loves rugby and will play anywhere at any time for

any cause in the game. Always he gives of his best and tries his hardest, and he is a prototype of all that is right and proper in a modern rugby player. His sense of humour is dry, hiding a shrewdness that has been handed down by Scottish ancestry, but he is sincere and always grateful for help.

He is a fine fielder of the ball; a good punter with a torpedo kick, and a good tackler. Wilson has speed about the field and remains cool in moments of crisis. His proudest moments were captaining Scotland against England and South Africa in 1965, and the Barbarians against New Zealand in 1967. In this last match he was disappointed for he played extremely well at full-back but his place-kicking was just off target. Had he kicked a couple of goals, the Barbarians would have won deservedly, and in any case they merited a draw, but his last kick failed to find touch because his left leg slipped during the punt. Lochore gathered the ball and it was Steel who got the winning try. Wilson did not deserve this misfortune but he was never a lucky player. Others in the game have made many more mistakes but Dame Fortune has smiled kindly, and they have survived.

Wilson played well as a full-back in both Barbarian matches against the All Blacks in 1964 and 1967, but like the New Zealand full-back Scott of the late forties and early fifties, he never enjoyed good fortune as a place-kicker, although placing some superb goals during his career. Both worried about this occasional failure, but never revealed it in their general play. Wilson, like Scott, was quite fearless in going down to forward rushes or in making a tackle, and enjoyed side-stepping his way out of trouble or running the ball out.

An excellent talker about the game and a good correspondent, he answered hundreds of letters on tour, and revealed unique patience in dealing with all enquiries. His camera was always at his elbow and he took some excellent 'stills' in colour, entering readily for the 'Oscar'. His other sports are golf and athletics while he enjoys travelling and studying the playing and coaching methods in the game.

Of the modern game, he says, 'Most clubs play too many matches; the players would benefit more from fewer games and more team practices under coaches. A system of priorities is required among club, county and national sides, so that the better players have greater opportunities to practise together at representative level.'

Behind this sensible comment, Wilson appears to express the hope that his country, which he has served so well, will adopt the princple of national squad training and bridge the 'gap'. One thing is certain, Wilson will never lose his interest in the game or the people who administer and play it. He is truly an amateur rugby player who has always enjoyed playing.

R. M. Young

If one had to vote for the happiest rugby player of the last ten years, there would be several candidates for the honour but, as one would expect, the happiest hails from Ireland where the majority of really happy rugby players are born! He is a scrum-half or 'skrumskakel' who admits, with a twinkle in his eyes, 'My hobby is touring and playing rugby!', but this is not quite true, for he is an intelligent young man, now qualified as a dental surgeon and with his humanitarian approach will serve his profession and fellow-man extremely well.

The 27-year-old Roger Young of Belfast is one of the most likeable personalities in international rugby at the moment, deserving of the title, often much maligned and misused, of a 'sportsman and a gentleman', for Young is indeed, both. Come what may, on or off the field, Young remains unperturbed and even on his birthday finds time to think of others. As modest as they come, he possesses the quiet determination of a true Ulster protestant but is beloved by all Ireland in the game, and as much admired at Lansdowne

Road as he is at Ravenhill Park. Young loves rugby football and the game admires Young!

His is the last name in a long and formidable list of Irish international players but, certainly, not least with his tally of 21 caps and he could still make inroads into the leading Irish scrum-half's record of 28 appearances held by the immaculate Mark Sugden. Effective but unobtrusive, Young is a sound, tireless player who will never let the side down. He can be kicked, tripped, punched, rolled-over, buried and bruised, but will still resume smiling because he has one of the biggest 'hearts' in the game, proving the American maxim that to succeed in sport 'you've got to have heart!'

Once in South Africa, in East London, Young left the field with cracked ribs but the local doctor at the ground said he was fit enough to carry on and so Young trotted back holding his side. He carried on for a while, and was then forced to retire in great pain as Tom Kiernan substituted at scrum-half as a replacement. An X-ray examination at the local hospital soon revealed the real trouble and he was out for the rest of the tour. At that moment the Lions had no scrum-half as the other partner in Skrumskakels Limited, Gareth Edwards, was also out with a damaged hamstring. Before he left hospital to rejoin the touring party Young was asked by a rather attractive administrative assistant for details of his next-of-kin, and he replied, 'Gareth Edwards, skrumskakel, c/o British Lions Team', which caused much amusement to all concerned. Edwards was his inseparable companion on the 1968 tour, and so strongly did they support each other that they were christened 'The Twins'.

Young was born in Belfast in June 1943, the son of a business sales manager who had not been connected with rugby, and is one of three children—his brother teaching history at Campbell College and his sister married to Brian Marshall, who played full-back for Ireland against England in 1963 to break Kiernan's long run of successive appearances. He attended Methodist College where he developed his skills at the game and then entered the famous Queen's University to study dentistry. On entering the University he followed a long line of Ulster undergraduates who have played such an important part in the history and development of Irish rugby.

Young was eleven years of age when he first played rugby football and I feel this is the best time of all to start to play the game, even though boys start much younger in New Zealand and other countries. Young was captain of Methodist College in 1961-62 and of the Ulster Schools, and was captain of Queen's in 1967-68. By 1965-66 he had achieved most honours in the game.

He first played for Ireland in 1965 after experience with Ulster, the Irish and British Universities which gave him a taste for touring. There followed the Wolfhounds and the Barbarians, before the British Lions of 1966 to Australia and New Zealand. Yet for Young his proudest moment will remain 'putting on the Irish jersey for the first time before the start of the French match in 1965 at Lansdowne Road, Dublin.' The match was drawn; it was a hard and tough game and a stern 'baptism' for the undergraduate, but he survived and remained first choice for Ireland in his position except, of course, when injured.

He was a delightful member of the 1966 Lions and even when he lost his Test place to Welshman, Allan Lewis, in New Zealand he remained the same likeable, modest, enthusiastic young man who put the team first at all times. This approach endeared him to all, for nothing was too much trouble for him. He was shy and happy, always respectable and sincere, and looked a grand sight in the saddle of a horse 17 hands high, riding through a West Coast town wearing a cowboy hat. Young was game enough to take part in all activities and his spirit could never be subdued.

As he told me on many occasions, 'I really enjoy touring with rugby teams, for the lads are great company. However, I enjoy sailing, tennis, squash, swimming and even a little non-professional rugby, while I am not averse to a little social ornithology!' Young enjoys playing and the grade of the jersey he wears does not affect the standard of his play for he is always trying hard. A dour defender and good punter of the ball, he has a long swinging service and occasionally bursts to the blind side or links up with his back row forwards. He is a remarkably clean player and rarely, if ever, retaliates, preferring to leave that to others, and whenever Young is injured, most of his colleagues crowd round him to find if there had been any illegal play causing the injury. When it has been so, the Irish and Lions players have admonished the opposing side's culprit.

He studies the game closely and he feels it is now more attractive to play and watch, due to the 'new dispensation about not kicking to touch outside the '25' line'. Young also believes that organised coaching is now producing results in all grades and, as a player in Belfast and Ulster competitions, agrees wholeheartedly that competitive club rugby produces a higher standard of teamwork.

To hear him singing in the corner of a lounge in some faraway country; to see his happy smile; to listen attentively to his delightful Ulster accent, and to watch him play with such enthusiasm and suffer without protest in the non-stop position of scrum-half is to realise that he is the happiest of players. However, in addition, Young is also a very good player, as not many poor ones appear for Ireland, especially at scrum-half, since Mark Sugden set the pattern!

PART FIVE

The Press

O. L. Owen

A sportsman and a gentleman; this is an accolade awarded to few in sport, but one such a man was the late Owen Llewellyn Owen, the respected and honoured anonymous chief rugby writer of *The Times* from 1913 to 1955. To me he was the ideal rugby critic; a man of dignity and sincerity who embodied fairness and accuracy in all his reports, yet possessed of a delightful sense of humour, without which he would not have succeeded or earned the respect and admiration of the rugby world.

I first met him in the happy years before the War and treasured the moments I was able to sit behind him in Welsh Press boxes and listen to his words of wisdom and humorous asides during his visits to Wales. Naturally, he attended international matches and top club matches as well as the annual Barbarians' Easter Tour. Like myself now, he was then broad in the beam and felt very much like a sardine in its proverbial tin while wedged into a favourable seat at the Cardiff Arms Park or St. Helen's. How often can I remember him saying, 'Thomas, the Welsh Rugby Union must do something about this Press box!' And, of course, he was right, but much too polite to attack the august body in print.

To him the game came first and its players received top priority in his writings. Again, although he was an admirable critic, one of the best in an era which boasted many great ones, he was primarily a first-class journalist in every way. He was trained in a hard and exciting school as a youngster, under the autocratic Northcliffe régime, and his tales of those early days kept me entranced for many an hour after World War II, as we travelled together often to international matches in Paris, Edinburgh and Dublin.

I recall one famous trip by the night ferry to France when he described one special 'job' as a reporter in covering the last public execution in France, and like a true 'Madame Defarge' and her creator, Charles Dickens, he described the scene in gory detail. In the corner of the bar of the cross-Channel steamer, I can see him now, with his eyes aglow, describing how the blood spurted from the headless body after the guillotine blade had fallen upon its victim. On retiring to bed and trying to sleep, every clank and mechanical noise sounded to me like a falling guillotine, and that night it was a restless ride to Paris!

Another famous story was that of his being sent to France to cover the first motor car thieves. They had robbed a bank and made their 'getaway' by car to set a new problem for the police; it was, indeed, the forerunner of a series of fantastic robberies as a result of the introduction of the internal combustion engine. All these fascinating yarns indicated the vast experience of O.L.O. as a journalist, and the meticulous care he took in his writing is an object lesson to all of us who write about the game.

He loved personalities, and amusing characters on the football field impressed themselves upon his exceedingly reliable memory. Jammy Clinch was a man he liked and admired because he gave colour to the game and made writing about him a pleasure. O.L.O. was not a static thinker in rugby football and moved readily with the changes in the game, studying and analysing them closely. He was deeply interested in the game in the Commonwealth, although he was never presented with the opportunity of travelling overseas, for not until 1962 did *The Times* send its Rugby Correspondent with a Lions side. Yet the 'Man from *The Times*' was quoted throughout the Commonwealth, and his comments and opinions were rated highly by administrators and players in distant lands.

He grew impatient only when sides and players did not perform the basic skills correctly, and was always keen to

Stewart Wilson.

J. W. Telfer (*right*) in action for the British Lions against Australia
at Sydney 1966.

Left: Reg Sweet. *Right:* Wilfred Wooller.

Vivian Jenkins and the Author.

observe good scrummaging. I recall him saying at the end of the 1951-52 season, 'Thomas, if the Welsh pack had scrummaged really well this winter, it would have been one of the greatest of Welsh sides since the "Golden Era".' O.L.O. watched many matches during the glorious era of Welsh rugby but grew unhappy in his later years about the lack of attention paid to the art of scrummaging. He had no time for players who were prima donnas and praised only those who contributed something worthwhile or who were always trying hard, and he cannot be faulted for this.

He did not confine himself to rugby football, for the gentle art of self defence was very dear to his generous heart and he described fights in which great performers like Jimmy Wilde, Jim Driscoll, Freddie Welsh, Georges Carpentier and others took part, while he was equally qualified to write about athletics and covered six Olympic Games. Yet, unlike so many young writers today, he was never dogmatic and did not profess at any time to 'know it all'. Perhaps there was little for him to learn in the post-War years, but his admirable enthusiasm, modesty and genuine love of sport, found him as good a listener as he was a talker.

With a rich-sounding name like Owen Llewellyn Owen, he was bound to have his share of Welsh blood although born in Ipswich, and he worked in South Wales as well as the West Country before migrating to Fleet Street and the popular dailies before moving to *The Times* at Printing House Square in 1913. He served that paper until 1955 but during his retirement acted at Editor of *Playfair Rugby Annual* and wrote with skill and profound knowledge for many periodicals as well as contributing to the literature of the game a book that will honour his name, *The History of the Rugby Football Union*. It was a labour of love but an invaluable effort, and when he died in February 1965 at the age of 78 he was missed dearly by those who knew and admired him. He was the last of the 'Great Three', who have yet to be replaced.

D. R. Gent

David Robert Gent was a little man with a big heart, a generous heart, and was the kindest critic that ever contributed a report of quality on the game of rugby football. To sit beside him was a pleasure; to know him and be helped by him was a privilege; and to read his weekly report of two columns in the *Sunday Times* between the wars was an education in the game. The impish face wreathed in smiles with head tilted to one side, could win the heart of the hardest forward or cheer the soul of the most disappointed administrator. Everyone loved 'Our Dai', the Welshman who played for England because none other than the legendary Dickie Owen kept him out of the Welsh XV in the 'Golden Era' of the game in the Principality.

In a moving tribute to the 'little man' of the Press Box, after his death in January 1964 at the age of 81, Vivian Jenkins, who succeeded him at the *Sunday Times*, wrote: 'Tiny of frame, as befitted the old-time school of scrum-halves, he exuded good cheer and kindliness and loved the game with a passion that reflected his early upbringing.'

Born in the Carmarthenshire town of Llandovery, he became a scrum-half, but found that he could not gain a regular place in the Swansea side because of the presence of the 'master' of the era, R. M. 'Dickie' Owen, one of the greatest of all scrum-halves.

So he set off into England to achieve a teaching diploma at Cheltenham College before taking a post at Gloucester to acquire dual qualifications for both England and Wales. While there it is recorded that he played in a trial for Wales against Owen, and later in the season was capped for England in January 1906 against Dave Gallaher's All Blacks. His choice came 'out of the blue' and was a real surprise, but he could not prevent England from losing the match at Crystal Palace by five tries to nil, and Gent's admiration for

New Zealand rugby players remained considerable for the rest of his life.

He played against Wales and Ireland in the same season and opposed Owen, of Wales, in the scrum-half position at Leicester, again on the losing side. R. T. Gabe once told me, 'Dai was a plucky player and tireless, but was wise to accept the inevitable because, good though he was, he could not match the remarkable Dickie Owen.' In saying this, Gabe was not being uncharitable, but indicating the greatness of Owen, and not any weakness on the part of Gent.

The Irish match was also lost and Gent lost his place, but he continued to play effectively for Gloucester and the County and after a long wait of four years returned to the England side in 1910 following his playing in the Rest XV which defeated the England XV at Twickenham in the first final trial played at the ground. When he was chosen to play for England against Wales in the first international at the new headquarters of English rugby in January 1910, Gent achieved two ambitions.

The first was to partner the illustrious Adrian Stoop, then at the zenith of his quite remarkable career and secondly, but equally important, was to play in the first England side to defeat Wales in 12 years. Gent was overjoyed because Owen and other illustrious players were in the Welsh side that day. His last international appearance was in the next match against Ireland, which was drawn, before giving way to A. L. H. Gotley, of Oxford University, who made six consecutive appearances.

Gent stood 5 ft. 3 in. and weighed 9 st. 7 lb., and few smaller men have played for their country, or even their country of adoption. In 1912 he helped Gloucestershire to win the County Championship, and then took a leading part in Cornwall, where he became deeply engrossed in coaching. After World War I he joined the *Sunday Times* in 1919, as a free-lance contributor, while continuing in his scholastic profession as a headmaster in Maidstone.

For 36 years he served the paper and the game faithfully

as a critic of quality and devotion, for he loved the game deeply and understood it easily. He kept young in heart by keeping pace with the game's continual process of change. Gent understood the inevitability of progress for better, for worse, and although he recalled the glorious days of pre-1914 and admired the England sides of the 1920's, he never looked down, cynically, upon the players of his later years, for he admired them, too, as exponents of the finer arts.

Having sat with him through many important matches in the late 1940's, I learned the art of criticism and express hope that a little of the kindness he showed towards all men was not lost on myself. His criticism was always fair, especially of younger players, and rather than be harsh he would conveniently ignore those performers below form.

Gent believed that rugby football is a blend of vigour and skill, restraint and risk but that, in the years before his death, it had become confused in its process of development. He felt that the forwards were neglecting the classical 'close' or 'tight' play and showing a preference for joining the backs in open play. As always, he believed the 1905 All Blacks to be the originators of 'mixed' play and that no side has played it as effectively since those remarkable fellows. He could be right!

However, he believed that two changes in his lifetime were bad for the game. First, the reduction of the dropped goal's value from four to three points and, secondly, the introduction of the advantage law which, though morally right, too often 'keeps the game in a suspended state of animation'. However, he felt that the game was more widely promulgated after World War II compared with his playing days of 1903-1913, when it was learnt 'by example', although he worried that the game would become too technical. He could be right in this, but he will be remembered always as an unrivalled judge of the game in company with O. L. Owen and J. P. Jordan during their lifetime. They were the 'Big Three' of the Press Box and set a new standard of rugby reporting.

J. P. Jordan, O.B.E., M.C.

Colonel John Paul Jordan was a worthy member of the great trio of rugby writers who dominated the years between the two world wars, and who did much to maintain the standard of the game, encourage players and popularise it through the columns of the papers of which he was a contributor, and they included the *Daily Mail, Daily Telegraph, Sunday Dispatch* and *Sunday Times*. When he became a free-lance after World War II, he wrote under his own name and three *nom-de-plumes*, John Paul, John Rivers and Dark Blue, which on analysis were quite clear!

Jordan was born in 1883, the son of a Hong Kong stockbroker, and was educated at Dulwich School and later St. John's College, Oxford. He was an excellent all-round sportsman and played scrum-half for his college with skill before joining the Old Alleynians, after leaving Oxford, and captaining the 'A' side. At the end of his career as a rugby player, the First World War arrived and he joined the Inns of Court Rifle Brigade to start a distinguished career as a soldier.

Jordan was commissioned in the Royal Artillery and served for most of the War in France, attaining the rank of acting-Brigadier, and winning the Military Cross, the Belgian Croix de Guerre and the French Legion of Honour. Not content with serving his country bravely and well on the field of battle, he joined the Territorial Army when hostilities ceased and remained in it until 1926. However, he returned in the 1930's and when World War II arrived he was given charge of a gun battery on the South Coast. For his services he was awarded the O.B.E.

A remarkably loyal man in every way with a quiet sense of humour; few were aware of the fact, apart from his closest friends, that his wife was an invalid for the greater part of their married life and that he was devoted to her in every

197

way. Colonel Jordan was a kindly gentleman of the 'old school' and gave a touch of dignity to the Press Box. Short, dapper, precise and deeply understanding of the game, he was an ideal critic, for his accuracy of detail gave authority to his writings.

As Rupert Cherry, of the *Daily Telegraph*, remembers him: 'J.P., as he was known everywhere, was a gentleman and the kindliest man I ever met in my profession; one who would always share his vast knowledge of rugby football with others and never made the others feel small when he did so.' There could be no better tribute than this to a professional critic.

Jordan never attempted to be a spectacular writer in his reports for he was content to provide balanced comment, with a shrewd judgment of the players and their tactics, plus an accurate report of the run of play. He never entered into heated argument; neither was he dogmatic in approach, but he loved the game deeply and safeguarded its interests by adhering to his basic beliefs. If he had any bias it was for Oxford University, but this is understandable and could be forgiven easily since he was so fair a judge. University and county football were very dear to his heart and he wrote with understanding also of club football, revealing admiration for those who played the game in the best traditions.

He wrote for magazines and, with Howard Marshall, compiled an invaluable addition of the rugby library. *The Story of the University Rugby Match*, which has become a standard work of reference on university rugby. Jordan, until his death in November 1956 at the age of 73, watched every Inter-Varsity match from 1898 onwards and Marshall comments, 'The research was extensive and mainly done by Jordan, most indefatigable and knowledgeable of rugby chroniclers and historians, and without his vast knowledge, records and memories, it would not have been perhaps possible and certainly less enjoyable.'

In all 'J.P.' watched over 250 international matches and I still retain many of his reports as records of value and interest.

He was a professional critic and an inseparable friend in the Press Box of Owen and Gent. When organising the Press seats at home internationals in Wales, I always contrived to put them together, in the years after the war, and listened to their chatter during matches.

I learned much from them and my respect for the 'great trio' remains. Players, who were criticised by them, revere their memory and the Barbarians of yesteryear will remember these dignified critics at Penarth on Easter tours. The game will not forget them and as one of many I owe them much for their help and guidance.

Eb Eden

A dapper, slim, humorous man and an extremely efficient, knowledgeable journalist, who for the greater part of his career (he retired in 1968) remained anonymous. Yet he was one of a small group of specialists who are the backbone of British newspaper production, the reporting staff of the Press Association. All who knew him and respected him as an important colleague in the Press Box, still admire Eb Eden, chief rugby correspondent for the Press Association from 1931 to 1968.

It is a long time in any journalist's career and Eb enjoyed every moment of it. In 1931 he took over rugby football and travelled round with Bennie Osler's formidable Third Springboks as they introduced a new brand of powerful forward play. They made a big impression upon the young critic with their accuracy, efficiency and match-winning qualities. Unlike Eb, they were serious in approach, but won all four internationals against strong sides.

His first international was the memorable one between Wales and South Africa at St. Helen's, Swansea, in December 1931, when heavy rain waterlogged the ground and, long before the end of the match, it was almost impossible to recognise the individual forwards. Eb survived this 'baptism' and covered every international for the next 37 years. In all he spent 51 years in Fleet Street and was born into a journalistic family. Eb's father owned a local newspaper at Wimbledon and his brother Guy can claim to be one of the best known and most respected of Parliamentary Lobby correspondents. Guy did duty for the Press Association, the *Daily Chronicle* and the *Daily Express,* and received the C.B.E. upon his retirement from journalism.

Eb's first job in journalism was that of a young telephonist with the Press Association and with him at the time were two young men who were to achieve fame in the profession, John Marshall of the London *Evening News,* and Louis Wulff who became the Press Association's Buckingham Palace man. Eb joined the P.A. Joint Service in August 1917 and, owing to shortage of staff, was 'pressed into service' as a night switchboard operator and later followed this as a telephonist and then as a junior sub. He followed with a short spell in the racing room before he joined Pardon's in May 1922.

Pardon's was the world's leading cricket agency and Eb became a partner in the company at the end of the Second World War. Now he has retired he still takes a keen interest in sport and the affairs of Fleet Street, and can often be found helping out in an emergency. His vast experience and knowledge of British sport enables him to judge quickly the value of a story and to recall any historic associations. He lives at Westcliff-on-Sea and one of his most interesting hobbies is that of stamp collecting, which he developed while on fire-watching duty at night during the London raids early in the War. Later he served as a special constable.

His views on rugby football are always sincere, interesting and analytical, and he believes that the match he most enjoyed writing about was that between Scotland and Wales at Murrayfield in 1951 when Scotland won by 19 points to nil because 'it provided one of the most notable instances of a triumph for the non-favourites. Wales had already swamped

England and in so doing produced such form that the Triple Crown looked as good as won. However, Scottish zest and enthusiasm completely upset their opponents and the score which caused the Welsh to fall apart was the second half dropped goal by Peter Kininmonth.'

Recalling the many players he watched as a critic he says the best and most exciting centre was Wilfred Wooller, of Wales, and adds, 'I thought him in every respect the complete centre. His long legs enabled him to cover ground at a remarkable pace and he often ran deceptively. He gave passes of top standard and seemed able to hold those of any quality. Moreover, his eye for an opening caused havoc among opposing defences as also did his powerful and astute kicking.'

Eb regards 'Tuppy' Owen-Smith as the full-back who afforded him the most thrills, as well as for his brilliance on the cricket field. 'I cannot recall any other player who displayed such readiness, even eagerness, to essay what looked to be the impossible and bring it off. There was never a dull moment when Tuppy was around.' His favourite outside-half was N. M. 'Nim' Hall and he says of him, 'For quick thinking and equally rapid translation of thought into decisive action, Hall had no equal.'

Eb says that despite the alterations to the laws of the game since 1823 it has remained, fundamentally, the same as it always was. 'There have been numerous tinkerings with the laws in rugby football, as in cricket, since World War II, all aimed at trying to counter the activities of certain smart alecs, who endeavoured to find a way round every effort to curb them. However, as the International Board has pointed out so frequently, changes in the laws are of no avail unless the players display the proper spirit. Beyond urging stricter refereeing on the big occasion, I am afraid I can offer no suggestion for gilding the lily. Let the players provide the solution!'

The best touring team in his experience were the 1951-52 Springboks under Basil Kenyon, which he rates higher than the 1967 All Blacks. He felt that Kenyon's team was the stronger and possessed the greater variety of attacking ideas. When asked how many internationals he had covered, he replied, 'I don't know, for I never kept a record!' Eb began his career as a comparative newcomer with the senior men in his profession, O. L. Owen, D. R. Gent, J. P. Jordan, Fred Dartnell, Leo Munro and Howard Marshall, and only gradually was he accepted as a member of the 'International Circus'. However, he soon became a regular opponent of Fred Dartnell at billiards and it was from this writer that he realised what the term,' flow of invective' really meant!

Everyone in the Press Box liked and admired Eb Eden, and Vivian Jenkins and myself have enjoyed many a Welsh 'story' retold by Eb with a pseudo Welsh accent. He was modest, accurate and most reliable in his reporting and he respresented all that was best in satisfying sports writing.

Terry McLean

The leading rugby writer in New Zealand at the moment is Terence P. McLean, of Auckland, known as 'Mac the Knife' and sometimes introduced by his colleague Gabe David, of Wellington, as 'Terry McLean will now sing!' He started out as a camp-follower in 1950 with the British Lions in New Zealand and since then has written millions of words following the All Blacks in Australia, South Africa, Rhodesia, Canada, France and the British Isles for his paper, the *New Zealand Herald* and its associated weekly.

In addition he has written for the Argus South African group, the N.Z. P.A., *The Times*, the *Sunday Telegraph*, *The Western Mail* and several other papers during his many tours. 'Mac' is criticised in his own land; he is criticised abroad, for his writing is individualistic and he likes to launch an 'exclusive' occasionally that shocks administrators to the very core! He is a newspaper man first and foremost, although he comes from a rugby family and his brother,

Hugh, was an outstanding All Black in the 1930's, touring with Jack Manchester's 1935 team in the British Isles. McLean often hits hard at the game at home and its governing body, the N.Z. Rugby Union.

When abroad he appears to include in his 'for home consumption' reports touches of pro-New Zealand and anti-opposition comment, but his writings for visiting consumption tend to be rather more diplomatic. He is indeed a rugby diplomat, who knows what his various groups of readers will enjoy!

The reader should not be mistaken, however, for McLean writes well; his technical knowledge is considerable and his style colourful. Again, he is a remarkably quick 'after-the-match' worker and never fails to lodge his cables in time. His ability to spot a 'story' is acute, as with the 'biting' row during the 1966 Lions' tour.

Mac enjoys illuminating 'off-the-field' stories in his books, like that of the 'great lover' report in his book of the 1965 Springboks' tour in New Zealand. This adds a certain spice to his writings and anecdotes, but could perhaps upset those players who are left to explain to anxious friends and officials when they return home!

However, he is an interesting travelling companion and enjoys a party, often rendering the old favourites, and especially Welsh hymns, in a strong, basso-profundo. He talks little in the Press Box and follows each match closely, unlike many colleagues who enjoy describing each move in detail long after it has happened. He watches referees closely and hallmarks unusual characters as 'jokers'!

McLean truly reflects the New Zealand approach to the game and, naturally, like Welshmen, wants his side to win, but praises readily, outstanding play by the opposition. His favourites down through the years have been Bob Scott, Tiny White and Colin Meads, and he has defended Meads violently on many occasions, but never more vehemently than after the 'sending off' incident at Murrayfield in 1967. He felt this deeply, as did all New Zealanders at the time,

but passions surely overruled their judgment in the heat of
the moment. How different from the O'Shea 'incident' of
1968 at Springs, when the British team management, captain
and Press, paid tribute to Referee Woolley instead of
castigating him as the New Zealanders did the immaculate
and sincere Kevin Kelleher.

Yet this is the New Zealand approach when defending
their own, for they do defend, by jove they do, and Terry
McLean, like his other colleagues, is in there, pitching as
determinedly as they fought in Italy with the New Zealand
Division. Indeed, their rugby is very much like a 'battle', on
and off the field.

McLean commits himself wholeheartedly, as do his country-
men at all times, and there is never any turning back. Again,
as a New Zealand Pressman he is privileged, for New Zealand
managers appear to tell them all, as they did after the Meads
suspension, while the British Press were handed a meagre
message from the Four Home Unions without any clarifica-
tion. New Zealanders stick together, on and off the field.

A happy family man, McLean is an excellent golf correspondent and deeply interested in the game himself—touring
New Zealand and Australian courses during the summer and
able to write with considerable knowledge on the game since
he is no mean player himself and has won many a 'dollar' on
the golf courses of the world.

Reg Sweet

One of the cheeriest and completely unflappable members
of the world's rugby Press boxes is ex-fighter pilot, more
British than the British, yet extremely loyal, South African,
Reg Sweet, of Durban, sports editor of the *Natal Daily News*.
He is an experienced journalist who has given a lifetime
of service to the respected Argus South African Newspaper
group and has done a considerable amount of good for the

game in his country and set a high standard of accuracy, fairness, humour and understanding in rugby reporting.

I first met him with the 1951 Springboks in Europe and this was easily the best touring team to visit the Northern Hemisphere since the War. It was a highly successful tour, easy and exciting to cover with outstanding management and remarkable players, and an ideal tour on which to cut one's teeth overseas. Watching the matches alongside Reg Sweet, was a pleasure and his amusing asides and War-time reminiscences generally released the tension, easily and quickly.

Then, when it came my turn to travel overseas to cover a rugby tour for the first time, there was a confidant, guide, helpmate, wise counsellor and friend waiting to greet me at the Riviera Hotel, Vereeniging. It was Reg Sweet and a friendship developed that I have enjoyed down through the years, while all British tourists and critics have come to respect and admire his writings.

In 1955 he christened the popular and delightfully sweet South African liqueur, Van der Hum—'Fanny's Bum', and the contrasting humour of Reg and that of Paul Irwin, quite the best sports columnist in the continent of Africa, kept the Press gang alert and happy. There was Jannie Beukas, Vic Holloway, Paul Irwin, Reg Sweet, Vivian Jenkins and myself, and we were joined later by Roy McKelvie, with Ace Parker and Geoff Clark operating for short periods when Beukas and Sweet developed mumps! This was the most compact and harmonious, not to say hilarious, Press party I have travelled with, and when Beukas and Sweet were stricken by the 'bug' in Aliwal North, the ex-R.A.F. gunner Beukas, who always flew without a parachute because of his cramped quarters, took to his bed with a friendly bottle of 'Ouidermiester' to battle it out, while Sweet, the ex-pilot, hired a single seater plane and flew home to Durban, where his charming wife and ex-War time nurse, nursed him back to health! Courage is a prominent feature of the Sweet make-up in a 'Raffles' sort of way, but he is the gentlest of men and not given to harsh words.

His writings are sincere and players accept his criticisms, almost with thanks. He is very much a 'Banana Boy'—a man of Natal—although born and educated in Cape Town. He has the breezy manner of Natalian rugby folk and is hospitable beyond normality; yet he will rarely relax until the job of work is done, this being the hallmark of a good journalist.

Sweet visited New Zealand and Australia in 1956, but then retired from overseas travelling before the 1960-61 Springbok tour of Europe, having visited the British Isles, France, New Zealand, Australia and the Argentine in his 10-year tour of duty. At the time his wife was ill and his three charming daughters needed father to care for them, and so he took to his desk as sports editor of the *Natal Daily News*, but has covered all the Test matches played in South Africa since 1960.

Another good friend, Ace Parker, took over the travelling job for the Argus Group and did it well until October 1968, when he, too, retired from the 'road' to become sports editor of the *Cape Argus*. Sweet and Parker are among the best rugby writers in the English language since the War and have put the game first at all times. Danie Craven has considerable admiration for both of them.

Phil Tressider

A young man of 19—making the big trip—a great adventure from his native city of Sydney as a 'cub' sports writer, found himself at the historic Stradey Park, Llanelli, in the midst of a controversial match. A player was ordered from the field by an international referee and for a while there existed a state of uproar. It was a severe test for such a young man and he reported it with all the vigour and inexperience of youth. He used raw, rich, searching adjectives and his descriptive words magnified the scene for his Australian readers.

The young reporter was Phil Tressider, now one of the world's most travelled cricket and rugby writers; the referee was Ivor David; the player was Australian, Colin Windon, and the match was Llanelli v the Wallabies. It set ablaze the tour of Bill McLean's 1947-48 Australian team in Europe and the memory of it still lingers. Phil Tressider cut his teeth on this tour and returned a little bitter about Wales and Welsh rugby men. Bill McLean felt the same and he said some hard things when he returned.

I remember the tour well, but Bill McLean, an outstanding player, forgave and forgot, and in 1966 I sat with him in his hotel at Brisbane when he said, 'It's all over now. Any Welshman is welcome here!' Phil Tressider, too, forgave quickly and we became friendly and still correspond regularly. In fact, he has made many visits with Australian rugby and cricket teams to the British Isles since 1947, and thoroughly enjoyed himself.

Now he writes with skill and penetrating analysis on cricket, rugby and golf while contributing to many of the world's leading papers. He has written many sports books that have been widely read and as the chief sports writer of the *Sydney Daily Telegraph*, he is rightly regarded to be at the top of his profession in Australia.

Phil has played most games, but now prefers golf and has a low handicap. However, he enjoys most writing about cricket and, like any genuine sports writer, he readily admits defeat if his own country is well beaten, never more so than when he stood champagne all round at St. Helen's, Swansea, in 1964, when Glamorgan first beat Australia!

Yet it is at rugby matches that I have shared most time with him and it was the superb comment at Melbourne in 1959 that I will remember longest. Peter Jackson and the British Lions had made a brilliant start to their tour and were gathering momentum. At the right moment, Tressider recalled what Charles Bray and Gerard Walter had said after the 1957-58 match between the Western Counties and the Wallabies at Bristol ... 'Wallabies go home!' Following a brilliant Lions try at Melbourne, Tressider, in the front row of the Press Box turned round to Vivian Jenkins and myself and said, 'Lions go home!' The wisecrack was much appreciated and has become a password between us. It revealed Tressider's sense of humour and behind the smiling, dry, wise-cracking façade is a sincere and kindly man, who is ready to help any colleague in distress. Not a great party man, he lives a comparatively quiet life, and often disappears while the Press parties are at their highest. Sport is his life and he has served it well.

Like most professional sports writers he has an admiration for the top sportsmen who are really genuine. His Australian favourite in rugby football is the globe-trotting Wallaby lock and prop-forward A. R. 'Tony' Miller, who, says Tressider, 'Is as well-known and respected on the fields of the British Isles, South Africa and New Zealand as he is in his home country. A record number of appearances in Test matches lay behind him and many an international opponent came to respect this fair-haired, bulldog prop-forward who gave and asked no quarter. Australia has found top-notch international for- wards all too scarce over the years, but in Tony Miller, O.B.E., the Wallabies had a champion trouper.'

Tressider feels that rugby football should be brought into line with the modern tempo and everything should be devised towards the achievement of greater continuity in the game. 'There should be spare footballs on the touch lines in Britain and smartly attired ball-boys assisting the touch-judges. I would like to see greater value given to the try. I would reduce the value of penalty and dropped goals to two points. I would dispense with flank forwards. Finally, I trust that the Australian touch-kicking dispensation has come to stay, for it is the greatest single factor in improving rugby football that has emerged during the decade.'

The side he has enjoyed most writing about were the 1952 Fijians that visited Australia and he says, 'Australia had never seen anything remotely like them before, for they were lithe, dusky, powerful giants who tossed the ball—and their luckless opponents—about in rollicking abandon. They produced record crowds and record gates and in Joe Levula, on the wing, they possessed one of the greatest players the position has known. Had he been born Welsh, French or South African, his fame would have been world wide.'

However, as a loyal Australian, Tressider regards scrum-half Ken Catchpole as the greatest player he has ever seen; a 'Champion among champions, a rugby pearl, who possessed the most alert of football brains and was always a 100 per cent team man. It was the saddest commentary on the game of rugby football that the future of this little champion should have been blighted by illegal play in a Test against New Zealand.'

Tressider will never condone anything that is unclean or unkind in sport, no matter how much he wants his own side or particular favourite to succeed. Travelling with various Australian rugby sides has enabled him to enjoy the heady glory of colourful success modestly, and suffer the pangs of defeat generously. His feeling for sport is deep and this is reflected in his writing, although he has a keen sense of news. Indeed, he enjoys recalling the day when his managing director telephoned him at midnight, and he was forced to get out of bed and visit a neighbouring hotel to check whether a Test cricketer had got married secretly! 'Thank goodness the cricketer concerned was a gentleman,' added Tressider with a smile.

Vivian Jenkins

When one has sat through more than a hundred Lions' matches with a friend and colleague, one can say, 'I know this man!' My ribs are still sore where his elbow has biffed me in exultation or disappointment as one British player has done well or another badly. We have travelled thousands of miles together by air, by road and rail, but only rarely by sea! We have dined and wined in most of the world's leading hotels; we have chatted with prime ministers, millionaires, charming ladies and famous players and administrators in many sports, as well as many characters in many countries. We have shared large rooms and small ones and visited many amusing places and, perhaps, best of all, we have watched some wonderful matches and players, attended some magnificent after-match parties and seen many of the wonders of the world, ancient and modern.

From Table Mountain to the Rockies, from Arthur's Seat to Bondi Beach we have travelled as a pair of rugby explorers and like poor Scheherazade, we can tell a thousand-and-one tales of our amazing adventures. There have been many happy days that have helped to keep us both young at heart, despite the late nights and early morning starts and the tremendous punishment we have survived from the hatchet men! On several trips our wives have travelled with us, revealing patience and understanding possessed by few charming women. They, perhaps, could tell stories about us that we would not want to tell ourselves, but all four of us appreciate the good fortune we have experienced as devotees of the wonderful game.

By now the reader will have guessed that my inseparable tour colleague and close friend is the former outstanding British Lion, Wales, Barbarian and London Welsh full-back, double Oxford 'blue' and distinguished *Sunday Times* correspondent, Vivian Jenkins. We have been setting off together since 1955 in search of the Game in many lands, and at the end of each long tour we have stepped off the plane at London Airport saying together, 'That'll be the last—we'll miss the next!' So far we have continued, gaining fresh enthusiasm with the start of each tour. We are addicts in our love of the game.

Travelling with Vivian Jenkins is an experience but mutual friends would regard this, probably, as the understatement of the year, for they wonder sometimes how we maintain our efficiency through five long months on the road. One needs stamina, and Vivian has this aplenty!

Son of a popular headmaster in a Vale of Glamorgan school, he was educated at Llandovery College, where he played rugby and cricket with enthusiasm and made both school teams at an early age. He moved on to read classics at Jesus College, Oxford, and achieved his double 'blue', playing in the centre at rugby and keeping wicket at cricket. In the inter-Varsity matches he distinguished himself with intelligent play and determination, but Wales elected to play him at full-back and the transfer was an immediate success. His first appearance for his country was at Twickenham in 1933 with many other new caps and Wales won a memorable victory under the leadership of Watcyn Thomas. Vivian quickly established himself at full-back and by 1938, when he toured with the British Lions in South Africa, he had achieved world rating. In the First Test at Ellis Park he and Gerry Brand established themselves as the greatest full-backs of their era. I will remember him, always, for his expert torpedo punting and his fine tackling, two hallmarks of a good full-back.

He retired from the game in January 1939 and joined the staff of the *News of the World*, to cover many sports for them, including motor-car racing, until he was called to the colours as a member of the Territorial Army in August 1939. Vivian played for the Army and Combined Services teams and in one of the greatest of British sides that represented the Army against France in Paris, in 1940. Demobbed in 1946, he returned to the *News of the World* and made two cricket tours with the MCC. Then he moved on to the *Sunday Times* to specialise in rugby football, following in the footsteps of the late Dai Gent, the kindest of all critics.

This move presented Vivian with the opportunity of writing in the manner he enjoyed best although he was still as kindly as his predecessor, to maintain the noble *Sunday Times* tradition. His experience in sport and his love and understanding of rugby football ensures his being able to analyse from the player's viewpoint. He is methodical and detailed in his approach and, of all my colleagues, the most insistent upon accuracy.

His ideas on the game are progressive and he believes implicitly in the need of the differential penalty. Having toured abroad regularly, he has chipped away continually for a change in the British approach. There is, too, a delightful sense of humour in his writings and touches of colour that add much to his essay-like weekly reports.

Two of his tours, those of 1955 and 1959, produced excellent books and though their writing taxed his patience, they were well worth the effort. Now he contributes to papers and magazines the world over and his opinions are widely read and respected.

When asked as to which match he has enjoyed most writing about, he answered without hesitation, 'South Africa v British Lions at Ellis Park in 1955, because of its "nail-biting" finish. At 23-22 to the Lions, South Africa could have won if their full-back, Van der Schyff, had converted South Africa's last try, in the closing seconds, before a record crowd, for Rugby, of 95,000. Van der Schyff missed, and we breathed again, but what a story it made!'

Of the many players who have given him pleasure to write about he names as the top three, Cliff Morgan, Tony O'Reilly and Peter Jackson, and he regards them as the most 'colourful' players on his six Lions tours, but names as runners-up Jeff Butterfield and Rhys Williams. It is interesting to note that all players were outstanding in the 1950's, the outstanding post-War days of British rugby.

Concerning the improvement of the game as a spectacle, he jumps readily on to his 'hobby-horse', which I feel, too, must become law in the not-too-distant future, for he says, 'Introduce the "differential penalty", and thus save between ten and fifteen minutes in nearly every match are taken up with kicks at penalty goals.'

Wilfred Wooller

It may take longer than usual to get to know Wilfred Wooller really well, for behind his extrovert sporting approach he is, basically, a shy and extremely modest man. Having known him for 30 years, I find him modest still, when talking about his own sporting achievements. That is why he is a good critic, for although he may reminisce in an article or report, he rarely, if ever, starts a piece, 'In my days we were better because...'

An extremely loyal friend and a lively companion in the Press Box, he reveals the authority of experience in his writing, having played rugby football and cricket with considerable success and tried his hand at soccer, golf, athletics, squash, hockey, tennis and many other games. Allied to this is a love of writing; of producing a fair, accurate, detailed and amusing report. I once heard an editor (not of Wilfred's paper) comment, 'I like the way Wooller says so much in 300 words!', which was a shrewd observation.

Wilfred enjoys talking and writing about cricket and rugby and is an excellent TV commentator and summariser on both games, although only rarely called upon these days. His cricket commentaries, though tinged naturally with the yellow daffodil of Glamorgan, are most knowledgeable, informative and amusing. He knows what he wants to say and says it!

His comments and forthrightness are more satisfying than the sixth form jargon that accompanies many of the modern Test match commentaries. After returning from a Japanese POW Camp he became secretary of Glamorgan CCC in 1946, and joined the *News Chronicle* as a writer on Welsh rugby affairs, following another Welsh international, the late Clem Lewis. Then he moved to the *Sunday Telegraph* after the sad demise of the *Chronicle*, and has written on rugby and cricket for the comparatively new paper with enthusiasm.

His sense of humour is often as critical as it is amusing, and he does not spare anyone if the honour and tradition of the two games he loves are at stake. Wilfred still feels that the games are for the players and if they enjoy themselves so will the spectators. The tenacity and determination he revealed on the rugby field for Cambridge University, Cardiff, the Barbarians and Wales, and on the cricket field for Glamorgan, Cambridge University and the Gentlemen of England, often highlight his writings, and while interested in politics and a staunch conservative himself, he abhors the introduction of politics into sport in any country.

One thing, however, he does regret and that is the duties of secretary of Glamorgan, which are now his first love in sport, have prevented him from travelling overseas since the War with any rugby touring team, while although he has never commented upon the fact, the MCC could have honoured him on at least one occasion with the captaincy of their side in Australia or indeed the management, a few years later.

When a player he was invited to tour with the British Lions in 1938, but business prevented it and South Africa missed the sight of a big, speedy threequarter in action. On the hard grounds of the Republic he would have become an even greater legend in the game. None who saw him will forget his greatest hour against New Zealand at Cardiff in 1935.

When I asked him recently about the match he enjoyed most writing about, he told me, 'Many are the matches a sports writer enjoys covering, and for a multitude of reasons. Sheer enjoyment at the skill of the players, or a tense struggle with much at stake, or a national meeting of note for one's country, or simply seeing a minority forecast coming good before one's eyes against odds. I would choose from many cricket and rugby memories for special comment the astonishing game won by Wales against England in April 1967 by 34 points to 21.

'It was such a complete contrast to the traditional

encounters between these two ancient rivals. Eight tries was more than the entire ration of my playing career against England and 55 points was very nearly a ration for a decade. It was exhilarating, carefree rugby which started like a snowball downhill. It gathered momentum and one could not stop it.'

When asked which was the player who had given him most pleasure to write about, he replied immediately, 'Haydn Tanner, whose career began in my era as a player and finished after I had joined the Press. Tanner was, in my view, the nearest player to perfection that I have seen. He made fewer mistakes in a long career than most players make in half a season. Two other players I have enjoyed writing about have been Cliff Morgan, who never let a game die on him if there was anything he could do to revive it. He was a great trier with tremendous ability, while Rhys Williams was a massive second-row-forward with intelligence and application.'

Wilfred holds firm views on the way the game should be played and as to how it can be improved. He feels every player should be made to learn the basic skills and, in particular, accurate passing. He would like the value of the penalty goal cut down by one of three methods—(a) creating the differential penalty, (b) narrowing the goalposts by four feet, and (c) increasing the value of a try. He would also like to see referees apply, more sternly, the off-side laws, especially the 10-yard law after a kick ahead, while he is adamant about the fact that all players joining a loose maul from the wrong side should be penalised, as well as those who do not release the ball, instantly, when tackled. Finally, he says club fixture lists should be limited to 40 matches a season. There is a lot of sense in these suggestions.

EPILOGUE

The Making of a Good Coach and a Good Captain

I have met several rugby personalities who have done much to influence my approach to the game and, strangely enough, two of them are New Zealanders! The first was R. T. Gabe, of Wales, who was my senior tutor, followed by 'Wakers' and his famous text book. Then came Danie Craven, the most intense of them all, followed by Jack Finlay and Victor Cavanagh, of New Zealand. Cavanagh I regard as the most clear-thinking of coaches and the man who first 'created' the ruck as we know it today, while Finlay was one of the shrewdest of coach-captains. But for Cavanagh and Finlay there may not have been a successful Fred Allen and the many recent All Black triumphs. To end this collection of views and memories, I invited Jack Finlay to talk about basic things in the game and recall that he was the vice-captain, No. 8, and pack leader of the 1945-46 Kiwis in Europe. What was employed by the Kiwis 25 years ago still holds good. Finlay is now a conscientious business executive, family man, expert gardener and fanatical follower of rugby, living in the small town of Fielding, near Palmerston North, in the North Island of New Zealand. A former All Black, selector and administrator, he is quite one of the keenest students I have met and, in his way, a 'disciple' of the surviving members of the 1905 All Blacks. His desire at all times—pefection!

J B G T : Upon what principle did you approach the game in 1945?

J F : Looking back over the years to 1945 is a long time! However, as one remembers, Charlie Saxton's coaching for the Kiwis was based on three principles—possession, position, pace—and he was lucky to have under his captaincy a bunch of young players who, possibly, had received little or no coaching. Thus, they had no preconceived ideas, but many had a great deal of natural ability. There were few players with pre-War provincial or better experience, and Saxton, Rhind, McPhail, Sherratt, Allen, Nelson and McLean, would be the total. Our aim was to win (as every team's purpose should be). Our approach was to play as well as we possibly could; keep to the principals of just simple rugby, and trust that such would see us through. We endeavoured to have every forward, to the extent of his natural ability, procure as quickly as possible the ball from the ruck (so very essential), line-out and scrum, and then pass it on to our talented back-line to do as best they could. In this we were very successful.

J B G T : Was there a basic pattern and any pre-match planning? Were opponents studied closely?

J F : Pre-match and after-match discussion and coaching were just on the principles of basic rugby; that is passing at the right time, correct backing-up, forwards all in behind the ball, team support (an essential), and individual effort only as part of this. I cannot recall any pre-match attention to the other side. Of course, we had very little chance of obtaining such information! The little word 'position' was so very important in our success. Once we had the ball (and to win possession was our main endeavour), players had to be in position, and always into position, as quickly as possible, more especially so when it is difficult to do so. If it is difficult for one of your players to get into position, it must be equally so for his opposite number, more so should he be the committed party (say having executed a tackle, stopped a dribbling rush or tackled a running forward).

J B G T : Was a disciplined approach adopted and how much were you able to dictate the pattern of play?

J F : The word discipline brings to mind the possible psychological reaction of the players. They were all in the army (and even in the New Zealand Army there was discipline), so discipline was part of the players' character. Most were very young and I feel their reaction to training and playing must have owed a lot, certainly, to this discipline. No discipline, however, as we saw it in many of the international teams of the 50/60's. I do not remember any indication of our team dictating the pattern of play. If we got the ball (and that was our intense purpose), we played with it to our best advantage. I do recall one game when different tactics may have produced a different result. This was the Newport game. The surface of the ground was patchy with one portion providing excellent footing and another portion all wet and slippery. We would get the ball; it would reach Jim Sherratt in the wet, where he would be tackled, for the ball to go loose, and then off would go Jim Hawkins the Newport scrum-half and his 'wolves'! I was captain on this day, and I should have brought Cook up to first five-eighths from full-back and got him to kick on to the good surface, and then by good passing, I am certain we could have won!

J B G T : What are the three basic qualities that go to make a successful side?

J F : First it is essential that the players must be fit and very keen. We will leave out the word 'dedicated'. They must be selected on character, and the quality of courage should be an essential. Of course, the more ability the players have the better the team should be. A team man is often preferable to a brilliant individual, unless all his talents are capitalised upon by his team-mates. In this I would mention Johnny Smith who, not only during the Kiwi tour, but in later years whenever he made a break, would be certain to give his outside an overlap and would be more than sure he gave an excellent pass. Not much, perhaps, but how essential. I would say that once you have the players it is not difficult for a good coach to turn them into an outstanding combination. To play rugby you must have the ball and it is the lack of this I feel has cost British teams success against New Zealand in 1950 and 1959. The most important one, of course, is the loose ball, or ball available as a result of a five eighths or centre or wing being tackled. When forwards go promptly to the ball it is to pick it up, if possible, but if not then it is heads down, binding with arms, eyes open, pushing forward and control the ball back. Speed is so essential. Shall we say, back tackled, forward arrives, one-two-three seconds, and if no ball by then, a side might as well not have it at all, for the opportunity is lost. This really is not difficult to do, but not done by British teams. This, if correctly understood, can be achieved very easily.

J B G T :   How great is the influence of captaincy?

J F :   I feel captaincy falls into two spheres: off the field and on it. Image, character and discipline are very essential parts of rugby. This, to me, really is the most important thing, for rugby really is a game of character and it is important that this be preserved. You would indeed be lucky to have a captain with all these qualifications and as well as proving himself a tactical captain. Again, if he is to be captain, his best position is at second five-eighth. From there he has an excellent view of the forward play (if he understands it), and should be in a position to dictate the policy of play, and amend or direct line-out and scrum deficiencies as he sees them. Closer in, you are 'closed in' and as General Montgomery would say, you are involved in the dog-fight, and not so well placed to amend or change the tactics. If needs be, tactics must be changed because a captain must direct and lead his side to victory!

J B G T :   All so simple; the theory of pattern play and what was good enough for the Kiwis, could be good enough for any side in any grade anywhere!

INDEX